Cooking at the C·I·A

(CULINARY INSTITUTE OF AMERICA)

BASICS   GRILLING   AMERICAN   ITALIAN   MEDITERRANEAN   HEALTHY   VEGETARIAN   HOLIDAY   SWEETS

RECIPES FROM THE PUBLIC TELEVISION SERIES

Cooking at the C·I·A

(CULINARY INSTITUTE OF AMERICA)

Produced by Marjorie Poore Productions

Photography by Alec Fatalevich

Contents

Introduction

When it comes to cooking, we can never stop learning. One of the best ways to broaden our culinary skills and recipe ideas is to uncover the secrets of the world's leader in culinary knowledge, the Culinary Institute of America (CIA).

Cooking at the CIA contains recipes from the fourth season of the popular public television series, "Cooking Secrets of the CIA". This book gives you the chance to explore Italian, American, and Mediterranean cuisines and to prepare quick and healthful meals. You'll expand your recipe collection with fresh, flavorful dishes, and menus.

Through our "Cooking Secrets" television series, and Cooking at the CIA, you'll learn how to add grilling techniques and quick recipes to your culinary repertoire—from Grilled Vegetable Medley with Chipotle-Sherry Vinaigrette, to Beef Tri Trip with Wild Mushroom Sauté, to Cod and Potato Fritters with Aioli—for everyday meals as well as for fabulous entertaining.

Although we're all watching our diets more than ever, one thing has remained constant: our appreciation for fine desserts. Perhaps as a reward for our increased interest in nutrition, we're treating ourselves to higher quality cakes, cookies, and pastries. In this cookbook, you'll find a varied selection of treats—from heart-healthy offerings to truly luscious creations—to satisfy the dessert lover in you.

Diversity of cuisine and cultures is evident in everything we offer at the Culinary Institute of America, and our public television series, "Cooking Secrets of the CIA", is no different.

The same expertise, experience, and quality that go into the CIA's curriculum were used to develop the recipes for the series and *Cooking at the CIA*. This series and its companion book bring the CIA classroom experience into your home, with the college's internationally acclaimed team of chefs and instructors sharing their ideas and knowledge while demonstrating some of their most intriguing and popular creations.

The CIA's respect for all cuisines is also evident in its range of on-campus restaurants. When the college opened the American Bounty Restaurant at its Hyde Park campus in 1982, it set the pace for the current worldwide popularity of regional American cuisine. Also in Hyde Park are the Escoffier Restaurant, which showcases modern interpretations of classic French cuisine; the Caterina de' Medici Dining Room, which features regional Italian fare; and St. Andrew's Café, the flagship of the college's pioneering efforts in nutritional cooking. Most recently, the Wine Spectator Restaurant opened at the CIA's continuing education campus in California's Napa Valley featuring the dishes of the Mediterranean prepared with the freshest ingredients.

Cooking at the CIA continues the CIA's fifty-year-long practice of upholding the principles of quality and substance in culinary education while keeping an eye trained on the future. Everything we do at the college is built on the twin pillars of tradition and innovation: our associate and bachelor's degree programs; the comprehensive continuing education courses designed for culinary professionals at our New York and California campuses; our instructional videotapes and books.

The public television program "Cooking Secrets of the CIA" and our book *Cooking at the CIA* are two more ways the Culinary Institute of America is carrying out its goal: to provide more opportunities for professionals and consumers alike to explore the compelling, exciting world of cooking.

So be prepared to have fun and bring delectable new creations to your table.

Basics

At the CIA, the training is technique based. That is, we teach our students basic cooking skills, such as sautéing, braising, roasting, and more, rather than just teaching them to follow recipes. Once our students master the fundamentals, they are able to use those skills when cooking anything—with or without a recipe.

In this chapter we offer dishes that illustrate some of these basic techniques. You'll learn to sauté, braise, and roast vegetables, poultry, and meats, as well as prepare mouthwatering accompaniments for each dish. It is our hope that you can use these basic techniques when making the other recipes in this book, as well as when you improvise in your own kitchen.

Grilling is an increasingly popular cooking method in this country. We devote an entire chapter to this new "basic" (see page 24).

Sautéed Sesame Squash

Sautéing vegetables is a quick way to get a healthy side dish on the dinner table. This version of sautéed squash is enlivened with fresh cilantro, Parmesan cheese, and sesame seeds.

2 tablespoons olive oil

1 red onion, diced

1 red bell pepper, diced

2 cloves garlic, finely minced

2 zucchini, cut into sticks (see Chef's Tips)

2 yellow squash, cut into sticks (see Chef's Tips)

1 tomato, peeled, seeded and chopped (see Chef's Tips)

2 teaspoons chopped fresh cilantro

2 tablespoons freshly grated Parmesan cheese

2 tablespoons sesame seeds, toasted

Salt and freshly ground black pepper to taste

SAUTÉ THE AROMATICS | In a large skillet, heat the oil over medium-high heat. Add the onion, pepper, and garlic and sauté for about 10 to 12 minutes, or until the onion is golden brown.

SAUTÉ THE SQUASH | Add the zucchini and yellow squash and sauté until the squash becomes soft, 4 to 5 minutes. Add the tomato and cilantro, and continue to sauté until the squash is slightly brown.

ADD THE REMAINING INGREDIENTS AND SERVE | Stir in the Parmesan cheese and sesame seeds. Taste and season with salt and pepper. Serve hot.

SERVES 6

➤ **CHEF'S TIPS**

To shorten prep time, you can cut the zucchini and yellow squash into sticks using the julienne disk of a food processor.

To peel and seed tomatoes: Core the tomatoes and cut through the bottom skin in the shape of an "X." Plunge the tomatoes, a few at a time, into a large pot of boiling water for 10 to 30 seconds (depending on ripeness). With a strainer, transfer the tomatoes to a bowl of ice water. Drain the tomatoes and peel away the skins with a paring knife. Cut the tomatoes in half (lengthwise if using plum tomatoes) and squeeze or scrape out the seeds.

Irish Lamb Stew

Though this stew is a classic example of braising lamb, the garnish vegetables are cooked separately and added to the stew at the end in order to retain their true textures and colors.

2 pounds boneless lamb stew meat, trimmed and cut into 1-inch cubes

1½ cups thinly sliced onions

1½ cups thinly sliced celery

¼ teaspoon fresh thyme leaves

Salt and freshly ground black pepper to taste

1 pound potatoes, thinly sliced

1½ cups shredded savoy cabbage

Worcestershire sauce to taste

1½ cups heavy cream (optional)

1 clove garlic (optional)

16 pearl onions, cooked and peeled

12 baby carrots, cooked

8 Brussels sprouts, cooked

8 new potatoes, cooked

Chopped fresh parsley for garnish

BRAISE THE LAMB WITH THE AROMATICS | Place the lamb in a flameproof casserole or Dutch oven and cover with cold water. Bring the water to a simmer over low heat, skimming the scum that rises to the top as necessary. When the scum has stopped forming, after about 20 minutes, add the onions, celery, thyme, salt, and pepper. Return the stew to a simmer and cook for 30 minutes.

SIMMER THE HEARTY VEGETABLES | Add the potatoes and cabbage to the pan, partially cover it, and continue to simmer until the meat is very tender, about 20 minutes. Strain the stew through a colander, catching and reserving the liquid in a bowl. Transfer the lamb to a clean casserole and keep warm.

MAKE THE SAUCE | Transfer the cooked onions, celery, potatoes, and cabbage to a food processor and process until they are smooth, adding a little of the cooking liquid if necessary. Return the pureed vegetables to the bowl with the reserved cooking liquid, and strain this mixture through a wire mesh sieve into a saucepan. Bring the sauce to a boil over medium-high heat. Taste and season with salt and pepper. Pour the hot sauce over the lamb and stir in the Worcestershire.

ENRICH THE SAUCE IF DESIRED | If desired, bring the heavy cream and garlic to a simmer in a saucepan. Remove and discard the garlic and stir the hot cream into the stew.

ADD THE VEGETABLE GARNISH AND SERVE | Stir in the pearl onions, carrots, Brussels sprouts, and new potatoes and heat through. Ladle the stew into soup bowls and garnish servings with parsley.

SERVES 4

➤ CHEF'S TIP
This stew thickens as it sits. Be sure that the sauce is very hot when it is added to the meat. Adjust the consistency if necessary by adding some broth, stock, or cream.

Sautéed Pork Medallions

Pork, onions, and apples are a classic trio, and here they are sautéed together for a quick, elegant entrée. Sautéed potatoes are a nice accompaniment.

Vegetable or canola oil

Flour

Paprika

1 pound onions, thinly sliced

10 tablespoons butter

10 thin apple slices, ½-inch-thick core removed

Ten 3-ounce pork medallions

Salt and freshly ground black pepper to taste

1 cup chicken broth

FRY THE ONIONS | In a heavy skillet, heat about an inch of the oil over medium-high heat until very hot. Place a small amount of flour in a shallow bowl and season with paprika. In batches, add the onions to the flour and toss well. Shake off the excess flour and carefully place the coated onions in the oil. Fry the onions until golden brown and drain on paper towels; set aside.

SAUTÉ THE APPLES | In another skillet, heat 4 tablespoons of the butter over medium heat. Add the apples and sauté until tender. Transfer the apples to a plate and keep warm.

DREDGE AND SAUTÉ THE PORK | Season the pork medallions with salt and pepper and dust with the flour mixture. Add the remaining 6 tablespoons butter to the skillet and melt the butter over medium-high heat. Add the pork medallions and sauté for about 3 minutes on each side, or until cooked through.

ARRANGE THE COMPONENTS ON A PLATTER | Arrange the pork medallions on a warm platter and arrange the apples decoratively on the side; keep warm.

MAKE A PAN SAUCE | Pour off the excess fat. Add the broth to the pan and bring to a boil, stirring to remove the browned bits from the bottom of the pan. Reduce the heat to low and simmer until the liquid is reduced slightly. Pour the pan juices over the pork medallions and top with the fried onions. Serve with the sautéed apples.

SERVES 5

Chicken Roasted Three Ways

Depending on your whim, a roasted chicken can be prepared in countless ways. Following are three methods of roasting a chicken with the same ingredients and slightly different roasting methods. Decide for yourself which method you prefer. Use an instant-read thermometer to check the doneness of the cooked chicken.

1 roasting chicken, about 3 pounds

1 teaspoon fresh thyme leaves

2 cloves garlic, peeled, but left whole

3 to 4 parsley stems

Salt and freshly ground black pepper to taste

1 onion, roughly chopped

1 carrot, roughly chopped

1 stalk celery, roughly chopped

Vegetable oil (optional)

SEASON AND TRUSS THE CHICKEN | Trim the chicken, rinse it well, and blot it dry with paper towels. Place the thyme, garlic, and parsley stems inside the chicken's cavity and season generously with salt and pepper. Truss the chicken with butcher's twine to hold the legs and wings in place.

ROASTING METHOD NUMBER 1 | Preheat the oven to 500°F. Place the chicken on a roasting rack so that it is resting on one side. Place it in the oven and roast for 20 minutes. Turn the chicken so it is resting on the other side and roast for another 20 minutes. Remove the pan from the oven and transfer the chicken to a plate. Scatter the onion, carrot, and celery in the roasting pan and set the chicken breast-side up on top of the vegetables. Return the chicken to the oven and roast for another 20 minutes, or until the thigh meat is cooked to an internal temperature of 180°F.

ROASTING METHOD NUMBER 2 | Preheat the oven to 350°F. Place the chicken in a roasting pan breast-side up on top of the onion, carrot, and celery. Place the chicken in the oven and roast until the thigh meat is cooked to an internal temperature of 180°F, about 1 hour and 15 minutes.

ROASTING METHOD NUMBER 3 | Preheat the oven to 350°F. In a large skillet, heat a small amount of oil over medium-high heat. Place the chicken in the pan and sear the chicken on all sides until golden brown. Scatter the onion, carrot, and celery in a roasting pan. Place the chicken breast-side up in the pan on top of the vegetables. Place the pan in the oven and roast until the thigh meat is cooked to an internal temperature of 180°F, about 1 hour.

REST AND CARVE THE CHICKEN | Remove the chicken from the oven and let stand for about 10 minutes before carving into serving pieces.

SERVES 2

Veal Shanks and Turkey Italian Sausage with Italian Cassoulet

This recipes shows how braising can be done in the oven, as well as on the stovetop. Cassoulet, the long-simmered bean and meat dish from France, is updated with Italian ingredients—Italian sausage, tomato sauce, and spicy pepper flakes.

4 pieces veal shank, about
4 to 6 ounces each

Salt and freshly ground black
pepper to taste

6 tablespoons olive oil, plus more
if needed

12 ounces turkey Italian sausage
links, cut into large chunks

3 medium onions, chopped

10 cloves garlic, minced

2 ounces pepperoni, finely diced

Fresh Tomato Sauce (recipe follows)

2 teaspoons dried oregano

2 teaspoons dried basil

1 loaf crusty Italian bread, cut
into 1-inch cubes

½ teaspoon red pepper flakes, or
more to taste

Cassoulet Beans (recipe follows)

Juice of ½ lemon

SEAR THE VEAL SHANKS AND SAUSAGE | Season the veal shanks with salt and pepper. In a Dutch oven, heat 2 tablespoons of the olive oil over medium heat until it just begins to smoke. Add as many veal shanks as will comfortably fit without overcrowding and cook until the shanks are browned on all sides; transfer the shanks to a platter. Continue cooking the shanks in this fashion until all are browned, adding a small amount of olive oil if needed. Add the sausage to the pan and sauté until browned on all sides; transfer the sausage to another platter.

PREPARE THE BRAISING SAUCE | Add the onions to the pot and sauté until translucent, about 8 minutes. Add the garlic and sauté it until its aroma is apparent. Add the pepperoni and sauté for 2 minutes. Add the Fresh Tomato Sauce, oregano, and basil and bring the mixture to a boil. Reduce the heat to low and simmer for 20 minutes.

BRAISE THE VEAL SHANKS | Preheat the oven to 325°F. Add the veal shanks to the Dutch oven and return the mixture to a simmer. Cover the pan and place it in the oven. Cook for approximately 1½ to 2 hours, until the veal is fork-tender.

SAUTÉ THE CROUTONS | In a large skillet, heat the remaining 4 tablespoons olive oil over medium heat. Add the bread cubes and toss them in the oil until well coated. Sauté the bread until the cubes are light golden brown on all sides. Transfer the croutons to a paper towel-lined platter.

ADD THE REMAINING INGREDIENTS | When the shanks have cooked through, stir in the sausage and pepper flakes, cover the pan, and return it to the oven for 15 minutes. Stir in the Cassoulet Beans and lemon juice. Taste the dish and season with salt and pepper.

TOP WITH THE CROUTONS AND BROWN | Increase the oven heat to 400°F. Top the cassoulet with the croutons and return the pan, uncovered, to the oven. Bake until the cassoulet is heated through, and the croutons are golden brown, approximately 15 minutes.

SERVES 4

Fresh Tomato Sauce

1 tablespoon olive oil

1 medium onion, cut into small dice

8 cloves garlic, minced

4½ cups peeled, seeded, and chopped plum tomatoes (see Chef's Tip page 8)

1 tablespoon chopped fresh basil

1 teaspoon lemon juice

Salt and freshly ground black pepper to taste

In a 2-quart saucepan, heat the oil over medium heat. Add the onion and sauté until translucent, approximately 6 minutes. Add the garlic and sauté until its aroma is apparent. Add the tomatoes and bring the mixture to a boil. Reduce the heat to low and simmer the sauce for 20 to 25 minutes. Add the basil and lemon juice and simmer for 5 minutes. Taste the sauce and season with salt and pepper.

MAKES ABOUT 5 CUPS

Cassoulet Beans

8 ounces dried great Northern beans, soaked overnight in water to cover by 3 inches

1½ teaspoons olive oil

2 medium onions, minced

8 cloves garlic, minced

1 large stalk celery, finely chopped

5 cups low-sodium chicken broth

1 bay leaf

3 sprigs thyme

1 small sprig rosemary

2 teaspoons salt

2 teaspoons freshly ground black pepper

Drain the beans, rinse them, drain them again, and set them aside. In a large saucepan, heat the oil over medium heat. Add the onions and sauté until translucent. Add the garlic and celery and sauté until the celery is tender. Add the rinsed soaked beans and enough broth to cover the beans by 1 inch. Bring the liquid to a boil over high heat. Reduce the heat to low and simmer the beans for 20 minutes. While the beans are simmering, skim any scum and oil that floats to the surface. Add additional stock to the beans as necessary to keep them from boiling dry.

Add the bay leaf, thyme, and rosemary. Continue to simmer the beans until they are just tender, approximately 1 hour, adding the salt and pepper after 30 minutes.

Chicken Provençal with Roasted Eggplant and Herbed Couscous

> The key to successful sautéing is to select the correct-sized pan. Choose one that will fit all your ingredients without having too much extra space, which will cause the food to burn, or too little space, which will cause the food to boil.

10 boneless chicken breast halves

All-purpose flour

Salt and freshly ground black pepper to taste

6 tablespoons vegetable oil

10 tablespoons unsalted butter

5 cloves garlic, minced

1¼ cups dry white wine

1¾ pounds peeled, seeded and chopped tomatoes (see Chef's Tip, page 8)

⅔ cup sliced black olives

3 anchovy fillets, mashed to a paste

2 to 3 tablespoons slivered fresh basil

Roasted Eggplant (recipe follows)

Herbed Couscous (recipe follows)

DREDGE THE CHICKEN BREASTS | Rinse the chicken breasts and pat them dry with paper towels. Place a small amount of flour in a shallow dish. Season the chicken breasts with salt and pepper and dredge them lightly in flour, shaking off the excess.

SAUTÉ THE CHICKEN BREASTS | In a large skillet, heat the oil over medium-high heat. Add the chicken and sauté until golden brown on both sides and cooked through (the internal temperature should reach 180°F). Transfer the chicken to a platter and keep warm.

MAKE THE SAUCE | Pour off the excess fat from the pan, add the butter, and heat over medium heat. Add the garlic and sauté for 1 minute. Remove the pan from the heat and add the wine. Return the pan to the heat and stir to scrape up the browned bits on the bottom of the pan. Stir in the tomatoes, olives, and anchovy paste, bring the mixture to a simmer, and cook it for 3 to 5 minutes to develop the flavors. Taste the sauce and season with salt and pepper.

GARNISH AND SERVE THE DISH | Return the chicken to the pan, along with any released juices that have accumulated on the platter, and stir to coat the chicken with the sauce. Heat until the chicken is warmed through. Divide the chicken among the serving plates and top with the sauce. Garnish servings with basil and accompany with Roasted Eggplant and Herbed Couscous.

SERVES 10

Roasted Eggplant

1 cup olive oil

½ cup balsamic vinegar

2 teaspoons finely minced fresh rosemary

6 cloves garlic, minced

Salt and freshly ground black pepper to taste

6 small eggplants

2 cups freshly grated Parmesan cheese

In a shallow baking dish, combine the olive oil, vinegar, rosemary, garlic, salt, and pepper. Cut the eggplant on the bias into ¼-inch-thick slices and place them in the baking dish with the marinade, tossing to coat the eggplant with the marinade. Let the eggplant stand for 30 minutes.

Preheat the oven to 450°F. Remove the eggplant from the marinade and place it on a rack on a sheet pan. Sprinkle the eggplant with the Parmesan cheese and roast for 15 to 20 minutes, until tender and golden brown. Serve hot or at room temperature.

Herbed Couscous

1½ quarts chicken broth

1 tablespoon olive oil

1 cup minced onions

4 cups instant couscous

1½ cups mixed minced fresh parsley and chives

Salt and freshly ground black pepper to taste

In a saucepan, bring the chicken broth to a boil. In another saucepan, heat the oil over medium heat. Add the onions and sauté until translucent. Stir in the couscous and herbs, mixing well. Add the boiling broth, salt, and pepper. Cover the pan and let the mixture stand for 10 to 15 minutes. Fluff the grains with a fork, taste, and adjust the seasonings. Serve hot.

Roasted Pork and Red Potatoes

Roasting is a method of "dry heat" cooking in which tender cuts of meat or poultry are placed uncovered in an oven without additional liquid. In this recipe a small amount of beer is added to the roasting pan to flavor the pan juices for the sauce.

2 ½ pounds pork butt

Salt to taste

One 12-ounce can dark beer

1 large onion, coarsely chopped

1 carrot, coarsely chopped

1 stalk celery, coarsely chopped

1 clove garlic, crushed

4 parsley stems

Salt water (see Chef's Tip)

½ teaspoon tomato paste

1½ cups chicken broth

Salt and freshly ground black pepper to taste

Roasted Red Potatoes (recipe follows)

PREPARE THE PORK FOR ROASTING | Preheat the oven to 450°F. Place the pork on a work surface and sprinkle it with salt. Pour three-fourths of the beer into a roasting pan and place the pork skin-side down in the pan.

ROAST THE PORK | Place the pork in the oven and roast for 20 minutes. Turn the pork skin-side up, and with a knife, score the surface of the pork in a diamond pattern. Return the pork to the oven and roast for 45 minutes, basting often with the pan juices.

ADD THE VEGETABLES | Add the onion, carrot, celery, garlic, and parsley stems to the pan and continue to roast for 10 to 15 minutes, or until the pork has an internal temperature of 160°F. Baste the surface of the pork with salt water. Remove the pork from the oven, transfer to a plate, and keep warm.

MAKE THE SAUCE | Add the remaining beer to the pan and stir to scrape up the browned bits. Stir in the tomato paste well. Add the chicken broth and simmer for 3 to 4 minutes. Strain the sauce and season with salt and pepper.

SERVE THE DISH | Cut the pork into slices and divide among serving plates. Drizzle the sauce over the top and accompany by Roasted Red Potatoes.

SERVES 4 TO 5

➤ CHEF'S TIP

For basting, mix salt into water until it tastes very salty on the tongue. Use this solution to flavor the pork and keep it moist during roasting.

Roasted Red Potatoes

1 pound red potatoes, peeled

Salt and freshly ground black pepper to taste

2 tablespoons olive, vegetable, or canola oil

1 tablespoon butter

Chopped fresh chives for garnish

Preheat the oven to 400°F. Season the potatoes with salt and pepper.

On the stovetop, heat the oil in a roasting pan. Add the potatoes and toss until the potatoes are well coated with the oil. Place the pan in the oven and roast for 20 to 30 minutes, or until tender. Add the butter and toss to coat the potatoes. Sprinkle with the chives and serve hot.

Beef Roulade with Braised Red Cabbage and Spaetzle

In German cuisine braising is a common cooking method, such as in this version of traditional *Rindsrouladen*—sliced beef rolled around a bacon, onion, and pickle filling. Braised red cabbage and spaetzle (tiny boiled dumplings) are apt partners.

¼ cup butter

4 ounces ham or lean bacon, cut into julienne

1 medium onion, cut into julienne

5 thin slices of beef round, 6 to 7 ounces each

Paprika

1 tablespoon mustard

½ cup julienned pickles, or to taste

2 to 4 tablespoons vegetable or canola oil

Salt and freshly ground black pepper to taste

1 medium onion, chopped

⅓ cup chopped carrots

⅓ cup chopped celery

1 teaspoon tomato paste

1½ tablespoons flour

6 tablespoons dry red wine

6 cups good-quality beef broth

Braised Red Cabbage (recipe follows)

Spaetzle (recipe follows)

SAUTÉ THE FILLING INGREDIENTS | In a skillet, heat the butter over medium-high heat. Add the ham or bacon and julienned onion and sauté for 1 minute; set aside to cool.

FLATTEN AND FILL THE BEEF ROLLS | With a mallet, flatten the beef slices until about ¼-inch thick and place next to each other on a work surface. Sprinkle the beef slices with paprika and spread evenly with mustard. Top the beef slices with the ham (or bacon) and onion mixture, dividing evenly. Top with the pickles. Roll the meat securely around the filling and tie with kitchen string.

SEAR THE BEEF ROLLS | In a large, heavy skillet or Dutch oven, heat the oil over medium-high heat. Season the beef rolls with salt and pepper, and add them to the pan. Cook the beef rolls in the oil until browned on all sides; transfer the rolls to a plate.

PREPARE THE BRAISING SAUCE | Preheat the oven to 400°F. Add the chopped onion, carrots, and celery to the skillet and sauté until browned. Return the beef rolls to the pan and stir in the tomato paste; cook for 1 minute. Add the flour and carefully stir until it is blended. Add the wine and stir to remove the browned bits from the bottom of the pan. Add the broth and bring to a boil.

BRAISE THE BEEF ROLLS | Cover the pan and place it in the oven. Braise for approximately 2 to 2½ hours, turning the rolls occasionally. Remove the pan from the oven and transfer the beef rolls to a warm serving platter; remove the strings and keep warm.

FINISH THE SAUCE | Strain the sauce into a clean saucepan and bring it to a boil over high heat. Reduce the heat to low and simmer until the sauce is reduced by one-third, removing any grease that rises to the surface. Taste and season with salt and pepper.

SERVE THE DISH | Pour the sauce over the beef rolls and serve warm accompanied by the Braised Red Cabbage and Spaetzle.

SERVES 5

➤ (recipe continues on following page)

Braised Red Cabbage

2½ tablespoons goose fat or vegetable oil

1 large onion, cut into julienne

2½ pounds red cabbage, shredded

Sugar to taste

2 tablespoons salt

1 medium apple, sliced

2½ tablespoons red wine vinegar

2 cups chicken broth or water

Sachet: 1 cinnamon stick, 1 small bay leaf, 1 to 2 whole cloves, and 5 crushed peppercorns, tied together in a cheesecloth bag

1 tablespoon red currant jelly

Lemon juice to taste

In a Dutch oven, heat the fat or oil over medium-low heat. Add the onion and sauté until translucent. Stir in the cabbage and cook for 3 minutes. Add the sugar, salt, apple, vinegar, broth or water, and the sachet and bring to a boil over high heat. Cover the pan, reduce the heat to low and braise for 35 to 60 minutes, until the cabbage is tender, stirring occasionally. Stir in the red currant jelly and lemon juice. Remove the sachet before serving.

➤ **CHEF'S TIP**
To save prep time, use the large-holed grating disk on a food processor to shred the cabbage.

Spaetzle

2 eggs

6 tablespoons milk

Salt to taste

½ teaspoon freshly ground black pepper, or to taste

¼ teaspoon freshly ground nutmeg, or to taste (optional)

1¼ cups flour

2 to 4 tablespoons butter

In a large bowl, combine the eggs, milk, salt, pepper, and nutmeg and mix well with a wooden spoon. Add the flour and stir until smooth. Let the dough stand for 10 minutes. With a spaetzle maker (or other shaping technique), drop the dough into a large pot of boiling salted water. Simmer the spaetzle until they rise to the surface of the water. With a strainer, remove the spaetzle from the water and place them in a bowl of cold water to stop the cooking. Drain the spaetzle well. When ready to serve, sauté the spaetzle in butter until heated through and lightly browned.

➤ **CHEF'S TIP**
Look for a spaetzle maker in a specialty food shop or department store.

Roasted Tenderloin of Beef with Roasted Vegetables

A perfect accompaniment to this elegant beef dinner is a pilaf made from a mixture of white and wild rice, and wheat berries. Cook each item separately and mix them together just before serving. Season the mixture with fresh thyme, salt, and pepper.

One beef tenderloin, about 3 to 4 pounds, trimmed (reserve the trim)

Salt and freshly cracked black pepper to taste

Vegetable oil

3 tablespoons minced garlic

3 tablespoons fresh thyme leaves

½ onion, chopped

½ carrot, chopped

½ stalk celery, chopped

¼ cup tomato paste

5 cups dry red wine

4 cups beef broth

Two 10-ounce packages pearl onions, peeled

2 pounds shallots, peeled

Cloves from 4 heads garlic

1½ pounds shiitake mushrooms, stemmed, caps cut into thirds

1 pound cremini (brown) mushrooms, stemmed, caps cut in half

1 pound white mushrooms, cut in half

1 pound oyster mushrooms, cut in half

1 tablespoon cornstarch, dissolved in water

2 cups mixed chopped fresh herbs

PREPARE THE BEEF FOR ROASTING | Season the beef with salt and pepper. Place a small amount of oil in a roasting pan and heat on the stovetop over medium-high heat. Add the beef and brown it on all sides. Transfer the beef to a baking sheet with a rack. Rub the beef with the garlic and fresh thyme.

PREPARE THE SAUCE | Add the beef trim to the roasting pan with the onion, carrot, and celery. Sauté over medium-high heat until the beef and vegetables are well browned. Add the tomato paste and cook until slightly browned. Add 2 cups of the red wine and stir to scrape up the browned bits from the bottom of the pan. Cook the mixture until it is reduced by half. Add the broth and cook until the mixture is reduced by half. After about 20 minutes, skim and discard the scum that rises to the surface of the liquid. Strain the sauce and set aside.

ROAST THE VEGETABLES AND BEEF | Preheat the oven to 425°F. Place another roasting pan on the stovetop. Add a small amount of oil to the pan and heat over medium-high heat. Add the pearl onions and sauté until they are slightly brown. Add the shallots and sauté until browned. Place the pan in the oven and roast for 15 minutes. Add the garlic and mushrooms and roast for 15 to 20 minutes. Add the beef to the pan and roast for 20 to 25 minutes for rare, to an internal temperature of 135°F. (For medium doneness, increase the roasting time to 20 to 25 minutes, 145°F; for well-done, increase the roasting time to 30 to 35 minutes, 170°F).

FINISH THE SAUCE | Remove the beef and vegetables from the roasting pan and keep warm. Add the remaining 3 cups wine to the pan. Place the pan on the stovetop and simmer until the liquid is reduced by half, stirring to scrape up the browned bits. Add the reserved sauce and heat through. Add the mushrooms to the pan and simmer for 15 minutes. Slowly stir in the cornstarch mixture and simmer, stirring, until slightly thickened.

SERVE | Cut the beef into serving slices and divide among warm serving plates. Divide the roasted vegetables among the serving plates and top with the sauce. Sprinkle with the fresh herbs and serve immediately.

SERVES 8 TO 10

Grilling

is a fashionable way to cook foods today. However, some find grilling's multitude of equipment and terminology confusing and intimidating. Here we offer a collection of recipes and careful instructions that will demystify grilling for the home cook.

There are a few main concepts to remember when grilling, weather on a charcoal, gas or electric grill. Think of the grill as an oven with added features. You have the option of grilling with two types of heat—direct or indirect—depending on the type of food you are cooking. As a bonus, you'll impart a smoky flavor to the food.

For direct heat grilling, center the food item grilling directly over the heat source and turn it during cooking—usually half-way through. Direct-heat grilling is a good method for small, sturdy cuts of meat or poultry that take less than 25 minutes to cook.

For indirect heat grilling, place the food to the side of the heat source, rather than directly on top. Cover the grill so that the air circulates around the food like a convection oven, which eliminates the need to turn the food during cooking. This method is useful for larger cuts of meats and poultry that take over 25 minutes to cook.

Grilled Cinnamon Chicken Skewers

Cinnamon sticks stand in for bamboo or metal skewers and infuse the chicken cubes with their distinctive flavor. This is a great dish to serve at a party, as it is easy to put together and is eye-catching on the plate.

6 boneless, skinless chicken breasts, about 3 pounds

Cinnamon sticks, split in half lengthwise

¼ cup prepared plum sauce

¼ cup sherry

1 tablespoon hoisin sauce

1 tablespoon soy sauce

3 green onions, green parts only, thinly sliced on the diagonal

2 tablespoons sesame seeds, toasted

COAT THE CHICKEN WITH THE SAUCE | Cut the chicken breasts into 2-inch cubes. Carefully thread the chicken onto the cinnamon sticks (you may have to make a hole in the chicken pieces with a knife in order to facilitate threading). In a large bowl, mix together the plum sauce, sherry, hoisin sauce, and soy sauce. Add the chicken skewers and carefully toss to coat the chicken with the sauce.

GRILL AND SERVE THE CHICKEN | Preheat the grill to medium-high (see page 41). Grill the chicken until it is cooked through, about 5 to 10 minutes. Transfer the skewers to a serving platter and garnish with the green onions and sesame seeds.

SERVES 6 AS AN APPETIZER

Grilled Vegetable Medley with Chipotle-Sherry Vinaigrette

Since the vegetables cook at different times, you can cook them in two ways: grill each type separately and keep warm until serving. Or, place the vegetable types on different parts of the grill and pay attention to the timing as they are cooking.

1 pound eggplant (about 1)

Salt

1 pound zucchini (about 2)

1 pound yellow squash (about 2)

1 pound portobello mushrooms

1½ pounds red bell peppers (about 3)

1½ pounds yellow bell peppers (about 3)

5 plum tomatoes

10 green onions

½ cup olive oil

Leaves from ½ bunch fresh thyme

Salt and freshly ground black pepper to taste

Chipotle-Sherry Vinaigrette (recipe follows)

CUT AND SALT THE EGGPLANT | Cut the eggplant into ½-inch-thick rounds, sprinkle it generously with salt, and let it stand in a colander for 30 minutes. Rinse the eggplant to remove the salt and blot it dry with paper towels, pressing to remove the excess moisture.

PREPARE THE REMAINING VEGETABLES FOR GRILLING | Preheat the grill to medium-high (see page 41). Cut the zucchini and yellow squash on the bias into long slices. Remove the stems from the portobellos. Cut the red and yellow peppers into eighths. Core and halve the tomatoes. Trim the root ends of the green onions.

GRILL THE VEGETABLES | In a bowl, combine the olive oil, thyme, salt, and pepper. Brush the vegetables with this mixture. Grill the eggplant, yellow squash, zucchini, and mushrooms for about 4 to 5 minutes per side. Grill the peppers for about 5 to 7 minutes per side. Grill the tomatoes and green onions for about 3 to 5 minutes. All vegetables should be tender, have nice grill marks, and be very hot.

ASSEMBLE THE DISH | Slice the portobellos to make 10 portions and divide among 10 serving plates. Arrange 2 to 3 slices each of eggplant, zucchini, and yellow squash on the plates. Add 2 strips each of red pepper and yellow pepper, a grilled tomato half, and a green onion. Drizzle the vegetables with the vinaigrette and serve warm or at room temperature.

SERVES 10 AS AN APPETIZER

Chipotle-Sherry Vinaigrette

¾ cup plus 1 tablespoon sherry vinegar

2 tablespoons fresh lime juice

4 chipotle chiles packed in adobo, minced (see Chef's Tip)

2 shallots, minced

2 cloves garlic, minced

1½ tablespoons pure maple syrup, or to taste

1 teaspoon salt, or to taste

½ teaspoon coarsely ground black pepper, or to taste

3 cups extra-virgin olive oil

½ cup chopped mixed fresh herbs, such as chives, parsley, tarragon, and chervil

In a large bowl, combine the vinegar, lime, chipotles, shallots, garlic, maple syrup, salt, and pepper. While whisking, slowly drizzle in the oil. Just before serving, mix in the herbs. Taste the dressing and adjust with maple syrup, salt, and pepper, if necessary.

MAKES ABOUT 4½ CUPS

➤ CHEF'S TIP
Actually smoked jalapeños, chipotles are often found canned or in jars packed in *adobo*, a tangy, dark red sauce similar to barbecue sauce. Look for chipotles in adobo in a Latin American market or specialty food store.

Pine Needle-Smoked Turkey Carpaccio

Wood chips and pine branches lend an intriguing flavor to thinly sliced smoked turkey drizzled with a tangy orange vinaigrette. We use the tender fillet of turkey breast meat with the same tapered shape as the beef tenderloin from the original Italian version.

Hardwood chips for smoking, such as hickory, mesquite, or apple

Pine branches (see Chef's Tip)

4 turkey tenders

Salt and freshly ground black pepper to taste

4 tablespoons olive oil

2 shallots, diced

½ cup balsamic vinegar

¼ cup orange juice

1 teaspoon honey

Juice of ½ lemon

Boston Lettuce

Shaved Parmesan cheese

Toast points for accompaniment

PREPARE THE SMOKING MEDIUM | Preheat the grill to medium-high (see page 41). Place a cast iron pot on the grill and fill it with a ¼-inch layer of wood chips. Add a layer of pine branches and top with a sheet of perforated aluminum foil.

SMOKE THE TURKEY | Season the turkey tenders with salt and pepper and place them on top of the foil. Cover the grill and smoke the turkey for up to 30 minutes, or until the internal temperature reaches 180°F. Remove the turkey tenders from the grill, wrap them tightly in plastic wrap, and place them in the freezer until semi-frozen.

PREPARE THE DRESSING | In a skillet, heat 1 tablespoon of the oil over medium heat. Add the shallots and sauté for 2 minutes. Add the vinegar, orange juice, and honey and bring to a boil. Cool the mixture and refrigerate until chilled. Taste the dressing and season with salt and pepper. Add the lemon juice and the remaining 3 tablespoons olive oil and blend well. For a creamier consistency, emulsify the dressing with a stick blender.

ASSEMBLE THE DISH | Remove the turkey from the freezer and remove the plastic wrap. Cut the turkey tenders diagonally into very thin slices. Arrange the lettuce in the center of a platter or serving plates. Fan the turkey decoratively on top of the lettuce. Drizzle the dish with the dressing and garnish with Parmesan shavings. Accompany with the toast points.

SERVES 4 TO 6

➤ CHEF'S TIP

If there are no pine branches in your area, substitute rosemary leaves or stems. Be sure to rinse the branches well and shake off the excess water.

Jerk Chicken Legs

Jerk is a Jamaican seasoning blend that flavors meats or poultry prior to grilling. Typically very spicy, jerk consists of a blend of onions, garlic, chiles, and spices, but the formula varies from cook to cook.

2 teaspoons ground allspice

1 bunch green onions, cut into ½-inch pieces

Leaves from 1 bunch fresh thyme

2 tablespoons grated fresh ginger

1 teaspoon freshly ground black pepper

½ teaspoon freshly ground nutmeg

1 teaspoon ground cinnamon

3 tablespoons vegetable oil

3 to 6 Scotch bonnet or habenero chiles, seeded, ribs removed (see Chef's Tip)

2 tablespoons minced garlic

1 tablespoon salt

¼ cup lime juice

½ cup orange juice

12 chicken leg-thigh portions

Sliced green onions for garnish

Flat-leaf parsley leaves for garnish

MAKE THE WET JERK RUB | In a food processor, combine all the ingredients, except the chicken, and process to a fine purée, adding only the amount of chiles to suit your taste. Store the rub in a covered container in the refrigerator until needed, no longer than 1 week.

MARINATE THE CHICKEN | Place the chicken in a baking dish. Wearing plastic gloves, rub the chicken generously with the jerk rub. Cover the dish and refrigerate for 24 hours.

GRILL THE CHICKEN | Preheat the grill to medium-high (see page 41). Place the chicken on the grill and cook, turning, for about 12 to 15 minutes, or until cooked through. The internal temperature should be at least 180°F. Serve sprinkled with green onions and parsley leaves.

SERVES 6

➤ CHEF'S TIP
Scotch bonnet and habanero chiles are among the hottest chiles available. Take care when handling them: Wearing plastic gloves, cut the chiles in half lengthwise. Place the chiles on a cutting board and with a paring knife, cut out the stem, seeds, and ribs.

Grilled Shrimp and Pineapple with Adobo de Achiote

This makes a perfect starter for a summer patio party. If using bamboo skewers, be sure to soak them in water for at least 30 minutes before using; this helps keep them from burning while grilling.

3 tablespoons achiote seeds (see Chef's Tip)

1 tablespoon allspice berries

2 teaspoons whole black peppercorns

1 tablespoon dried Mexican oregano

2 tablespoons cider vinegar

Juice of 3 limes

6 cloves garlic, roughly chopped

1 tablespoon salt

1 cup vegetable or olive oil

72 large shrimp, peeled, deveined, tail-on

72 chunks pineapple

48 small red onion wedges

Guacamole (recipe follows)

Salsa Cruda (recipe follows)

Leaves from 1 bunch fresh cilantro

MAKE THE ACHIOTE PASTE | Place the achiote seeds, allspice, peppercorns, oregano, vinegar, limes, garlic, salt, and oil in a blender and puree until a very smooth paste forms. Pour the paste into a shallow pan.

ASSEMBLE AND MARINATE THE SKEWERS | On each of 24 skewers, thread 3 shrimp, 3 pineapple chunks, and 2 red onion wedges, alternating ingredients. As you assemble the skewers, place them in the pan with the achiote paste, turning the skewers to coat them evenly. Let the skewers marinate for at least 1 hour before cooking.

GRILL THE SKEWERS | Fifteen minutes before you're ready to cook, preheat the grill to medium (see page 41) and brush the grates to clean them. Place the skewers on the grill and cook for about 2 to 3 minutes per side, until the shrimp are just cooked through (take care not to overcook the shrimp).

GARNISH AND SERVE THE SKEWERS | Place the skewers on a serving platter and serve hot or at room temperature with the Guacamole and Salsa Cruda. Garnish the platter with cilantro.

MAKES 24 SKEWERS

➤ **CHEF'S TIP**

Achiote seeds, from the annatto tree, are popular ingredients in Latin American cuisine. They lend an unique flavor and yellowish-red color to recipes. Look for rusty red seeds—they're fresher than dull brown seeds—in a Latin American market or the international aisle of a high-quality supermarket.

Guacamole

10 ripe avocados, halved, pitted,
and peeled

Juice of 2 limes, or to taste

1 cup diced tomato (optional)

1 jalapeño chile, minced

1 bunch green onions, sliced

¼ cup chopped fresh cilantro

1 teaspoon Tabasco sauce, or to taste

Salt and freshly ground black pepper
to taste

Combine all the ingredients in a food processor and pulse until the desired consistency is achieved. For a chunkier consistency, mix the ingredients by hand. Taste the guacamole and adjust with lime juice, Tabasco, salt, and pepper. Transfer the guacamole to a storage container, cover tightly, and refrigerate until ready to serve. It is best to make guacamole the same day it is to be served.

MAKES ABOUT 1 QUART

Salsa Cruda

2½ cups seeded and diced tomatoes
(see Chef's Tip, page 8)

½ cup minced onion

½ cup diced green bell pepper

2 cloves garlic, minced

½ cup chopped fresh cilantro

1 teaspoon chopped fresh oregano

Juice of 2 limes

1 jalapeño chile, seeded and minced

2 tablespoons olive oil

¼ teaspoon ground white pepper, or
to taste

2 teaspoons salt, or to taste

Combine all the ingredients in a food processor and pulse until the desired consistency is achieved. For a chunkier consistency, mix the ingredients by hand. Taste and adjust the seasonings. Refrigerate until ready to serve.

MAKES ABOUT 1 QUART

Smoked Shrimp and Avocado Quesadillas

Like a hot Mexican sandwich, quesadillas consist of a savory filling wrapped between tortillas, which are grilled or fried and served warm. This version features a paste of smoky charred tomatillos mixed with creamy avocados and spices, topped with smoked shrimp. A watercress salad with orange vinaigrette is a nice counterpoint.

1 onion, diced, and sautéed until golden

½ pound tomatillos, charred, husks removed (see Chef's Tip)

2 avocados, pitted, peeled, and diced

¼ bunch fresh cilantro, chopped

1 tablespoon cumin seeds, toasted

Salt and freshly ground black pepper to taste

20 six-inch flour tortillas

½ pound Monterey Jack cheese, shredded

2 tablespoons olive oil

Smoked Shrimp (recipe follows)

2 bunches watercress, washed and dried

Orange Vinaigrette (recipe follows)

MAKE THE TOMATILLO PASTE | Place the onion, tomatillos, avocado, cilantro, cumin, salt, and pepper in a food processor and pulse to form a coarse paste.

FILL THE TORTILLAS | Divide the tomatillo-avocado mixture among 10 tortillas, spreading evenly. Top each tortilla with the cheese, dividing evenly. Place the remaining 10 tortillas on top of the cheese, lining up the edges. This process can be done up to 1 hour in advance of serving.

COOK THE QUESADILLAS | Lightly brush one side of each quesadilla with the oil. In batches, place the quesadillas in a nonstick skillet, oiled-side down, and cook over low heat until golden brown. Brush the other side with oil, turn over, and cook until golden brown. Keep the quesadillas warm in a low oven until all are cooked.

GARNISH AND SERVE THE QUESADILLAS | Cut the quesadillas into quarters and place on serving plates. Top each quesadilla with 4 Smoked Shrimp. In a bowl, toss the watercress with the vinaigrette to taste and divide the dressed greens among the plates. Drizzle the perimeter of the plates with some of the remaining vinaigrette.

SERVES 10 AS AN APPETIZER

► CHEF'S TIP

Tomatillos resemble small green tomatoes that are wrapped in a papery brown husk. They can be found in better supermarkets or in Latin American markets. To char tomatillos, place them directly in a gas flame or over very hot coals until the papery husks are black. Peel and discard the husks.

You can also cook these quesadillas on a medium-hot grill.

Smoked Shrimp

2 pounds large shrimp, peeled and deveined

Hardwood chips (apple, hickory, or mesquite)

Place the shrimp in salt water (the water should taste salty on the tongue) and soak for 30 minutes; drain well. Preheat the grill to high (see page 41). Place a layer of hardwood chips in an aluminum pan and position a rack on top. Place the shrimp on the rack and cover the pan tightly with foil. Place the pan on the grill and cook the shrimp for about 10 minutes. Immediately remove the shrimp from the pan to prevent overcooking.

MAKES 2 POUNDS

Orange Vinaigrette

½ cup orange juice

¼ cup white wine vinegar

¼ cup lemon juice

2 teaspoons Dijon-style mustard (optional)

3 cups light olive oil or canola oil

2 teaspoons salt

½ teaspoon freshly ground black pepper

3 tablespoons minced fresh herbs, such as chives, parsley and/or tarragon (optional)

In a bowl, combine the orange juice, vinegar, lemon juice, and mustard, if using. While whisking, gradually drizzle in the oil until blended. Season the dressing with salt and pepper and stir in the fresh herbs, if desired.

MAKES ABOUT 1¼ CUPS

Spit-Roasted Duck with White Beans and Beet-Orange Salad

> This recipe utilizes the rotisserie feature of a gas or electric grill. The Asian-style glaze that coats the duck turns it a rich, dark brown color as it roasts on the spit. Succulent white beans and a tangy beet and orange salad are lovely companions.

1 cup orange juice

½ cup soy sauce

2 tablespoons grated fresh ginger

2 cloves garlic, minced

1 duckling, about 4 to 5 pounds

1 sprig parsley

6 sprigs thyme

6 sprigs cilantro

1 bay leaf

Wood chips, soaked

1 tablespoon grated orange zest

¼ cup chopped fresh cilantro

Salt and freshly ground black pepper to taste

PREPARE THE MARINADE | In a small bowl, combine the orange juice, soy sauce, ginger, and garlic; set aside.

CLEAN AND MARINATE THE DUCK | Remove the giblets from the duck cavity, reserving the neck and gizzard. Rinse the duck inside and out and pat it dry with paper towels. With a knife, remove the wings at the second joint and set them aside. Trim any excess skin and fat from the duck and reserve it. With the knife, score the skin on the duck breast with ⅛-inch-deep cuts. Place the duck in a large locking plastic bag with the marinade, shake to coat the duck well, and refrigerate it for 2 hours.

SPIT-ROAST THE DUCK | Preheat a gas or electric grill with a rotisserie attachment to medium-high (see page 41). Remove the duck from the marinade, reserving the marinade. Stuff the duck cavity with the parsley, thyme, and cilantro sprigs, and the bay leaf. Truss the duck and place it on the spit of the grill's rotisserie attachment according to the manufacturer's directions. Adjust your grill to medium heat and add wood smoking chips as recommended by the manufacturer. Roast the duck until it is tender, approximately 1½ to 2 hours; the internal temperature should reach 180°F.

BASTE THE DUCK | Twenty minutes before the duck was finished roasting, bring the marinade to a boil in a small saucepan. Cool the marinade slightly and stir in the orange zest and chopped cilantro. Taste the marinade and adjust the seasoning with salt and pepper. During the last 15 minutes of roasting, brush the duck with the marinade every 5 minutes. If necessary, turn up the heat of the grill to crisp the duck skin and render any excess fat. Remove the duck from the grill and allow it to rest for 20 minutes.

CARVE AND SERVE THE DUCK | Carve the duck into serving pieces and divide it among 6 plates. Accompany it by the White Beans and Beet-Orange Salad.

SERVES 6

White Beans

½ pound dried white beans,
soaked overnight in water to
cover by 3 inches

3 to 4 cups duck or chicken broth

1 duck neck and gizzard (reserved
from Spit-Roasted Duck)

2 duck wings (reserved from Spit-
Roasted Duck)

1 bay leaf

1 whole clove

Duck fat and skin (reserved from
Spit-Roasted Duck)

1 carrot, cut into small dice

½ white onion, cut into small
dice

1 clove garlic, minced

½ cup peeled, seeded, and diced
tomato (see Chef's Tip, page 8)

1 teaspoon fresh thyme leaves

Salt and freshly ground black
pepper to taste

1 tablespoon white wine vinegar

Drain and rinse the beans and place them in a large pot. Add 3 cups of the broth, the reserved duck neck, gizzard, and wings, the bay leaf, and clove. Bring the liquid to a boil over high heat. Reduce the heat to low and simmer until the beans are tender, approximately 1½ to 2 hours, adding more broth as needed to keep the beans submerged.

While the beans are cooking, place the reserved duck fat and skin in a small saucepan and cook over low heat. When approximately 2 tablespoons of fat have been liquefied, discard the skin and solid fat pieces. Add the carrot to the pan and sauté until nearly tender, approximately 6 minutes. Add the onion and garlic to the pan and sauté until the onion is translucent, approximately 5 minutes.

Remove the duck parts from the beans and add the carrot mixture, tomato and thyme. Simmer the mixture for 5 minutes. Taste the beans and adjust the seasonings with salt, pepper and vinegar.

➦ (recipe continues on following page)

Beet-Orange Salad

4 red beets, greens trimmed to
1 inch

4 golden beets, greens trimmed to
1 inch

2 tablespoons white wine vinegar

2 teaspoons grated orange zest

¼ cup fresh orange juice

Salt to taste

Pinch of cayenne pepper

5 tablespoons extra-virgin
olive oil

3 navel (seedless) oranges, peeled
and sliced into thin rounds

Preheat the grill to medium-high (see page 41). Wrap the beets with foil, place them on the covered grill, and roast them until they are fork-tender, approximately 1 hour, depending on the size. While the beets are roasting, combine the vinegar, orange zest, orange juice, salt and cayenne in a medium bowl. While whisking, slowly drizzle in the olive oil until incorporated.

When the beets are cool enough to handle, trim them and slip off the skins using a paring knife. Slice the beets into rounds and add them to the bowl with the dressing while still slightly warm. Toss the beets well to coat with the dressing and let them stand at room temperature for at least 30 minutes. Just before serving, add the oranges and toss well.

Barbecued Sirloin with Grilled Oysters and Grilled Broccoli

Almost any food can be cooked on the grill, as this recipe shows. Shellfish, such as oysters, are delicious when grilled, as the smoke flavors from the fire are a nice complement to the delicate, briny flesh of the shellfish.

2 teaspoons pure chile powder

2 teaspoons ground mace

1 teaspoon ground nutmeg

1 teaspoon salt

1 teaspoon sugar

1 teaspoon freshly ground black pepper

3 teaspoons onion powder

2 teaspoons garlic powder

1 teaspoon dried thyme

1 teaspoon mustard seeds

¼ teaspoon ground cloves

1 teaspoon dried orange peel

2 pounds top sirloin

2 tablespoons olive oil

12 oysters in half shell

Chili Sauce (recipe follows)

1 pound broccoli with stems, blanched (see Chef's Tip)

Salt and freshly ground black pepper to taste

Crushed coriander seeds to taste

Vegetable oil spray

SEASON THE STEAK | Preheat the grill to medium (see page 41). In a bowl, mix together the chile powder, mace, nutmeg, salt, sugar, pepper, onion powder, garlic powder, thyme, mustard seeds, cloves, and orange peel. Rub the steak with the spice mixture and let stand for 5 minutes.

GRILL THE STEAK | Brush the seasoned steak with the oil and grill, turning, until cooked as desired, about 6 to 8 minutes for medium-rare (145°F) or 8 to 10 minutes for well done (170°F).

GRILL THE OYSTERS | Top the oysters with a small spoonful of the Chili Sauce. Place the shells directly on the grill and cook for 5 to 10 minutes, until the oysters are just barely cooked and heated through; take care not to overcook the oysters.

GRILL THE BROCCOLI | Season the broccoli with salt, pepper, and coriander. Spray the seasoned broccoli with vegetable oil spray and place on the grill. Cook the broccoli for 5 to 6 minutes, until tender-crisp.

SERVE THE DISH | Slice the steak and divide it among 4 warm serving plates. Place 3 oysters on each plate and accompany with the grilled broccoli.

SERVES 4

➤ CHEF'S TIP

To blanch broccoli or other dense green vegetables, bring a large pot of water to a boil. Plunge the broccoli into the boiling water and cook until the broccoli is about halfway done and is a vibrant green color. Drain the broccoli and immediately plunge it into a bowl of ice water to stop the cooking and cool it rapidly. Drain the broccoli and set aside until it's needed.

(recipe continues on following page)

Chili Sauce

6 tablespoons ketchup

4 tablespoons prepared chili sauce

1 tablespoon olive oil

1 teaspoon grated horseradish

Worcestershire sauce to taste

Tabasco sauce to taste

Lemon juice to taste

Combine all of the ingredients in a bowl and mix well. Let the sauce stand for at least 1 hour to blend the flavors.

► **CHEF'S TIP**
The following chart is useful for any of your grilling recipes:

TYPE OF HEAT	GAS/ELECTRIC GRILL TEMPERATURE	CHARCOAL GRILL APPEARANCE
Medium-low	325–350°F	Coals should have a heavy covering of white ash
Medium	350–400°F	Coals should be glowing red with a moderate covering of white ash
Medium-high	400–450°F	Coals should be glowing red with a light covering of white ash
High	450–500+°F	Low flames should still be visible within the coals

Grilled Lobster Tails with Angel Hair Pasta and Macadamia Nuts

Placed over a bed of pasta and julienned vegetables, and jazzed-up with Asian flavorings, this dish is a complete meal—a delightful new way to serve lobster tails. Macadamia nuts add a nice crunch.

Four 10-ounce lobster tails

2 tablespoons peanut oil

8 ounces angel hair pasta

1 tablespoon sesame oil

4 green onions, coarsely chopped

6 tablespoons balsamic vinegar

1 to 2 tablespoons brown sugar

1 teaspoon grated fresh ginger

1 teaspoon finely mashed garlic

½ red bell pepper, roasted and cut into julienne (see Chef's Tip)

½ yellow bell pepper, roasted and cut into julienne (see Chef's Tip)

½ green bell pepper, roasted and cut into julienne (see Chef's Tip)

⅓ cup crushed macadamia nuts, toasted

2 teaspoons sesame seeds, toasted

1 tablespoon chopped fresh chives

GRILL THE LOBSTER TAILS | Preheat the grill to medium-high (see page 41). Brush the lobster tails with the peanut oil and grill them for 8 to 10 minutes, or until they are cooked through. Transfer the lobster tails to a plate.

COOK THE PASTA | In 2 quarts of boiling salted water, cook the pasta until slightly firm to the bite, *al dente*, about 5 to 7 minutes. Drain the pasta and rinse with it cold water.

TOSS THE PASTA WITH THE REMAINING INGREDIENTS | In a large skillet, heat the sesame oil over medium-high heat. Add the green onions and sauté quickly. Add the vinegar, brown sugar, ginger, and garlic and remove from the heat. Add the julienned peppers and the pasta and toss well, until heated through.

GARNISH AND SERVE THE DISH | Divide the pasta mixture among 4 serving plates. Place a grilled lobster tail on each plate and sprinkle with the macadamia nuts, sesame seeds, and chives. Serve immediately.

SERVES 4

➤ CHEF'S TIP
To roast peppers or chiles, grill (or broil) the peppers or chiles until the skin is charred on all sides. Place in plastic bag or covered bowl until cool enough to handle. With a paring knife or your fingers, remove and discard the blackened skin, the stem, and the seeds.

Grilled Spicy Pork with Mango Salsa and Coconut Rice

Common in Jamaica, "jerked" foods are coated with a bold, chile-flecked seasoning mixture before grilling. Tangy mango salsa and nutty coconut rice complete the tropical theme.

JERK PASTE

¼ cup ground allspice

1 teaspoon ground cinnamon

1 teaspoon freshly grated nutmeg

5 green onions, roughly chopped

½ onion, roughly chopped

1 Scotch bonnet chile, stemmed and seeded (see Chef's Tip, page 30)

Salt and freshly ground black pepper to taste

2 tablespoons dark rum

¼ cup pineapple juice

2 tablespoons soy sauce

1 tablespoon salt

2 tablespoons vegetable oil

6 whole pork tenderloins

Vegetable oil

5 chayote squashes

1 pound carrots, cut into julienne

Salt and freshly ground black pepper to taste

¼ cup butter

Leaves from 1 bunch fresh cilantro

Coconut Rice (recipe follows)

Mango Salsa (recipe follows)

PREPARE THE JERK PASTE | Combine all the ingredients in a blender or food processor and process until smooth. You should have a thick but moist paste; set aside.

PREPARE AND SEASON THE PORK | Trim the pork of excess fat and sinew. In a skillet, heat a small amount of vegetable oil over high heat. Add the pork tenderloins and cook quickly until seared on all sides; cool. When the pork is cool enough to handle, rub it well with the jerk paste; set aside.

PREPARE THE VEGETABLES | Place the whole chayotes in boiling salted water and cook them until tender. Cool the chayotes in ice water and remove the peels. Remove the seeds and cut the chayotes into julienne.

GRILL THE PORK | Prepare a medium-hot barbecue fire or preheat the grill to medium-high (see page 41). Place the pork on the grill and cook, turning occasionally, for about 12 to 15 minutes, until the internal temperature is 170°F. Remove the pork from the grill and set aside.

SAUTÉ THE VEGETABLES | In a skillet, heat the butter over medium-high heat. Add the blanched chayotes and the carrots and sauté until the carrots are tender and the chayotes are heated through. Add the chopped cilantro and season with salt and pepper.

GARNISH AND SERVE THE PORK | Cut the pork into serving portions. Divide the chayote-carrot mixture among twelve serving plates and top with the pork. Accompany the pork with the Coconut Rice and top with the Mango Salsa.

SERVES 12

→ (recipe continues on following page)

Coconut Rice

2 tablespoons butter

2 cups long-grain white rice

3 cups water

2 cups unsweetened coconut milk

¾ teaspoon salt, or to taste

In a saucepan, heat the butter over medium heat. Add the rice and stir until the grains are coated with the butter. Add the water, coconut milk, and salt, and stir with a fork. Bring the liquid just to a boil, and reduce the heat so that the mixture simmers gently. Simmer the rice for approximately 16 minutes, or until the grains are tender. Fluff the rice with a fork to separate the grains.

Mango Salsa

One mango, about 10-ounces, cut into small dice

½ medium-sized red onion, cut into small dice

1 teaspoon minced jalapeño chile

2 tablespoons lime juice

½ teaspoon grated lime zest

2 tablespoons extra-virgin olive oil

2 tablespoons chopped fresh basil

1 teaspoon finely chopped lime zest

Combine all the ingredients in a food processor and pulse until the desired consistency is achieved. For a chunkier consistency, mix the ingredients by hand. Let the mixture stand for 1 hour to blend the flavors.

Tandoori-Style Chicken with Yogurt Masala

In India, tandoori foods are cooked on skewers in their name-sake oven, a deep clay oven that uses a very hot fire as its heat source. You can approximate this method at home using a very hot grill. Tandoori chicken is usually served with an assortment of fresh and preserved chutneys, and a "salat" of grilled onions and tomatoes, with wedges of lime on the side.

Three chickens, about 3 pounds each

Juice of 1 lemon

1½ tablespoons salt

1 cup plain yogurt

¼ cup water

2 teaspoons cayenne pepper

1 tablespoon ground cumin

1 tablespoon ground cardamom

½ teaspoon ground turmeric

3 teaspoons ground coriander

2 ounces fresh ginger, grated

4 cloves garlic, minced

6 tablespoons ghee (see Chef's Tip)

3 limes, cut into quarters

Assorted chutneys

PREPARE THE CHICKEN | Remove the skin from the chickens, leaving the birds whole. Cut the chickens into 4 serving pieces each, making 12 breast portions and 12 leg-thigh portions. With a sharp knife, cut a few ⅛-inch-deep slits in the breasts and thighs. In a bowl, mix the lemon and salt. Rub the salt mixture over the chicken, pressing the mixture firmly into the slits.

MAKE THE YOGURT MASALA | In a bowl, mix the yogurt, water, cayenne, cumin, cardamom, turmeric, coriander, ginger, and garlic until blended. Spread the masala (marinade) over the chicken and place it in a baking dish. Cover the dish and refrigerate for a minimum of 12 hours.

GRILL AND SERVE THE CHICKEN | Preheat the grill to high (see page 41). Remove the chicken from the dish, place it on the grill and cook, turning, for about 10 minutes, or until cooked through. The internal temperature should be at least 180°F. Baste the chicken occasionally with the ghee. Accompany the chicken with the lime wedges and chutney.

SERVES 6 TO 10

► **CHEF'S TIP**

Ghee, also known as clarified butter, is a common ingredient in Indian cuisine. It is actually butter from which all of the milk solids have been removed, leaving a pure, golden liquid fat. Since all of the impurities have been removed, ghee can be cooked at a much higher temperature than butter without smoking. You can find ghee in jars in Indian markets or specialty food stores, but it is easy to make yourself at home.

To make ghee: Place pieces of unsalted butter in a heavy saucepan. Melt the butter over low heat, without stirring, until it separates into layers; the milk solids will sink to the bottom. Skim the foam that rises to the top as the butter melts. Carefully pour or ladle the clear golden fat into a storage container; discard the solids and the milky liquid that remains on the bottom of the pan.

Grilled Beef Fillet with Chimichurri Sauce

Argentine in origin, chimichurri sauce is a common companion to grilled meats in that country. You might think of it as a variation of herb pesto, without the nuts, and flavored with vinegar.

4 to 6 cloves garlic, sliced

¾ teaspoon kosher salt, plus more as needed

⅓ cup water

⅓ cup extra-virgin olive oil

⅓ cup red wine vinegar

¼ cup finely diced red bell pepper

2 tablespoons minced onion

2 tablespoons minced fresh Italian parsley

2 tablespoons minced fresh oregano

1 small tomato, finely diced

1 jalapeño chile, minced

One beef tenderloin, about 3 to 4 pounds, trimmed

¼ teaspoon freshly ground black pepper

SOAK THE SKEWERS | Place several bamboo skewers in a pan of water and let stand for at least 30 minutes (this ensures that the skewers don't burn during grilling).

MAKE THE CHIMICHURRI SAUCE | In a food processor, combine the garlic, salt, water, oil, vinegar, bell pepper, onion, parsley, oregano, tomato, and jalapeño. Pulse the ingredients until a saucelike consistency is reached. To make by hand, mince the garlic. Sprinkle the salt over the garlic and mash it to a paste with the flat side of a chef's knife. Transfer the garlic paste to a glass or stainless steel bowl and add the water, olive oil, vinegar, red pepper, onion, parsley, oregano, tomato, and jalapeño; mix well.

GRILL AND SERVE THE BEEF | Preheat the grill to high (see page 41). Cut the beef into ½- by 1- by 2½-inch pieces. Thread the beef onto the soaked skewers and season the beef with salt and pepper. Grill the beef skewers until desired doneness, about 2 minutes per side for medium-rare. Serve with the chimichurri sauce.

SERVES 8 TO 10

American

food, like any other country's cuisine, is difficult to categorize. It is composed of different regions with many distinct cooking styles and unique indigenous ingredients.

Here we offer an assortment of recipes typical of many of America's regions, such as the Cajun-inspired foods of Louisiana, the chile-infused dishes of New Mexico, the seafood-packed cuisine of New England, and the fresh fruit and vegetable preparations of California.

Manhattan Corn Chowder

Borrowing an idea from Manhattan clam chowder, this soup incorporates tomatoes into its base rather than the cream of a New England-style chowder. Use homemade broth, or a good-quality low-sodium canned variety.

2 tablespoons olive oil

4 ounces bacon, finely diced

½ red bell pepper, finely diced

½ green bell pepper, finely diced

1½ medium-sized yellow onions, finely diced

3 cloves garlic, thinly sliced

2 stalks celery, finely diced

2 tablespoons minced fresh thyme

2 bay leaves

2 teaspoons dried oregano

2 cups fresh sweet corn kernels

2 cups small diced Yukon gold potatoes, or other boiling potatoes

2½ quarts chicken broth

1½ cups peeled, seeded, and diced tomatoes (see Chef's Tip, page 8)

Salt and freshly ground black pepper to taste

¼ cup extra-virgin olive oil for garnish

2 tablespoons coarsely chopped fresh Italian parsley for garnish

⅓ cup freshly grated Parmesan cheese for garnish (optional)

COOK THE BACON | In a 4-quart saucepan, heat the oil over medium heat. Add the bacon and cook until the fat renders and it begins to turn brown and crisp.

SAUTÉ THE AROMATICS | Add the peppers, onions, garlic, and celery to the pan and sauté over low heat until the vegetables are softened and the onions are translucent.

SIMMER THE SOUP | Add the thyme, bay, oregano, corn, potatoes and broth to the pan and bring to a boil over high heat. Reduce the heat to low and simmer until the potatoes and the corn are tender, about 20 minutes. Add the tomatoes and season the soup with salt and pepper.

SERVE THE SOUP | Ladle portions into heated bowls or soup plates garnished with olive oil, parsley, and Parmesan, if desired.

SERVES 12

➤ **CHEF'S TIP**
You can freeze the extra chowder after cooling it completely and placing it in a freezerproof container.

New England Corn Chowder

New England-style clam chowder is enriched with milk or cream. In this recipe corn chowder takes on the same guise, using half-and-half to give it body without adding too much fat.

2 tablespoons canola oil

4 ounces bacon, finely diced

1½ medium-sized yellow onions, finely diced

3 stalks celery, finely diced

2 bay leaves

2 teaspoons chopped fresh thyme

2 cups small diced Yukon gold potatoes, or other boiling potatoes

2 cups fresh sweet corn kernels

1 quart chicken broth

2½ cups half-and-half

Salt and freshly ground black pepper to taste

3 teaspoons whole butter for garnish

2 tablespoons chopped fresh Italian parsley for garnish

COOK THE BACON | In a 3-quart saucepan, heat the oil over medium heat. Add the bacon and cook until the fat renders and it begins to turn brown and crisp.

SAUTÉ THE AROMATICS | Add the onions and celery to the pan and sauté over medium heat until the onions are translucent and the celery is softened.

SIMMER THE SOUP | Add the bay leaves, thyme, potatoes, corn, and broth to the pan and bring to a boil over high heat. Reduce the heat to low and simmer until the potatoes and corn are tender, about 20 minutes.

ENRICH THE SOUP | Stir in the half-and-half, season with salt and pepper, and gently heat through.

SERVE THE SOUP | Ladle portions into heated soup plates or bowls garnished with ½ teaspoon of the butter for each portion, coarsely ground black pepper, and parsley.

SERVES 12

➤ CHEF'S TIP
If you want to freeze this soup, it's best to do so before enriching it with half-and-half. After thawing, heat the soup through, then proceed with the recipe.

Crab and Shrimp Gumbo

Though gumbo gets its name from a derivation of the word for okra, the vegetable is optional in this thick Creole-style seafood stew. Be sure to cook the roux, the mixture of flour and fat that thickens the stew, until it is very dark in color in order to achieve the right flavor.

2 pounds medium shrimp

2 tablespoons butter

10 crabs, cut in half

2 quarts chicken broth

⅔ cup vegetable oil

1 pound boneless, skinless chicken breasts, diced

½ pound spicy smoked sausage, diced

⅔ cup all-purpose flour

⅓ cup finely diced celery

⅓ cup finely diced green bell pepper

⅓ cup thinly sliced green onion tops

1½ cups chopped tomatoes

2 teaspoons dried thyme

2 teaspoons dried oregano

1 teaspoon ground allspice

1 teaspoon freshly ground black pepper

¼ teaspoon cayenne pepper

1 bay leaf

Salt to taste

Lemon juice to taste (optional)

Tabasco sauce to taste (optional)

PREPARE THE STOCK AND SHELLFISH | Peel, devein, and dice the shrimp. Reserve the shrimp shells and refrigerate the meat. In a large skillet, melt the butter over medium heat. In batches if necessary, add the shrimp shells and crab halves and sauté until the shells turn bright red. Add the broth and simmer for 20 minutes. Strain the mixture, reserving the broth and solids separately. Cool the broth. Pick the crabmeat from the shells and refrigerate the crabmeat; discard the crab and shrimp shells.

BROWN THE CHICKEN AND SAUSAGE | In a large soup pot, heat 2 tablespoons of the oil over medium-high heat. Add the chicken and sausage and sauté until browned. With a slotted spoon, transfer the chicken and sausage to a plate; set aside.

MAKE THE ROUX | Add the remaining oil to the pot. Stir in the flour and cook over low heat, stirring constantly, until the roux turns medium brown, about 20 to 30 minutes. Add the celery, green pepper, and green onion tops, and continue to cook, stirring, for about 10 minutes, until the roux is dark brown and the vegetables have softened and browned lightly.

SIMMER AND SERVE THE SOUP | Gradually whisk the reserved broth into the roux mixture. Stir in the tomatoes, thyme, oregano, allspice, pepper, cayenne, and bay leaf. Bring the mixture to a simmer and cook for about 45 minutes. Add the shrimp and crabmeat and simmer for about 5 minutes, until the shrimp is cooked. Taste the adjust the stew with salt, lemon juice, and Tabasco, if desired. Ladle the soup into soup plates and serve immediately.

SERVES 12

Spinach and Mustard Greens Salad with Malted Peanut Dressing

Mustard greens add spunk to this spinach salad studded with crisp jícama and sweet strawberries. The malt vinegar tames the bitterness of the mustard greens and the peanuts add crunch.

⅔ cup malt vinegar

1 teaspoon chopped garlic

1 tablespoon chopped fresh chives

1 teaspoon freshly ground black pepper

1 teaspoon dry mustard

2 tablespoons brown sugar

⅓ cup peanut butter

1¼ cups peanut oil

4 cups spinach leaves

2 cups young mustard greens

½ cup thin jícama strips

1 cup sliced ripe strawberries

½ cup sliced red onion

PREPARE THE DRESSING | In a bowl, combine the vinegar, garlic, chives, pepper, mustard, sugar, and peanut butter; mix well. While processing with a stick blender or whisking by hand, slowly drizzle in the oil until blended.

TOSS THE SALAD | In a large salad bowl, combine the spinach, mustard greens, jícama, strawberries, and red onion. Whisk the dressing and add about 1 cup to the bowl. Toss until the ingredients are well coated with the dressing. Serve immediately.

SERVES 4

➤ **CHEF'S TIP**
Any unused dressing can be kept in a tightly capped jar in the refrigerator. Whisk briefly before using.

Spinach Salad with Bacon Dressing and Hush Puppies

This version of spinach salad features crunchy enoki mushrooms and bright-red radicchio. The dressing features thickened vegetable stock to replace part of the oil. Hush puppies, usually served in the southern states with fried catfish, make a nice alternative to croutons.

8 ounces bacon, cut into small dice

3 tablespoons minced shallots

1 clove garlic, minced

½ cup plus 1 tablespoon brown sugar

6 tablespoons cider vinegar

6 tablespoons vegetable stock thickened with cornstarch (see Chef's Tip)

6 tablespoons vegetable oil

¾ teaspoon salt

¼ teaspoon freshly ground black pepper

1½ pounds spinach leaves, washed well

6 ounces enoki mushrooms

¼ pound radicchio, thinly sliced

30 Hush Puppies (recipe follows)

COOK THE BACON | In a skillet, cook the bacon over medium-high heat until it crisps and the fat is released (rendered); remove the bacon and set aside.

MAKE THE DRESSING | Add the shallots and garlic to the bacon fat in the skillet and sauté over medium heat until translucent. Add the brown sugar and stir until dissolved. Add the vinegar, thickened stock, and oil, and bring to a boil. Stir in the salt and pepper and keep warm.

MAKE THE SALAD | Place the spinach, mushrooms, and radicchio in a large bowl. Pour the warm dressing over the top and toss quickly until the spinach is slightly wilted.

SERVE THE SALAD | Divide the salad among 10 salad plates and garnish with the reserved bacon. Place 3 hush puppies on each plate. Serve immediately.

SERVES 10

> **CHEF'S TIP**

Using thickened broth to replace some of the oil in salad dressings reduces some of the fat in the dressing while adding flavor. It's a trick we use often at the St. Andrew's Café on our Hyde Park campus.

Place the broth in a saucepan and bring to a boil. Dissolve some cornstarch in water until it is the consistency of heavy cream. Add a small amount of the cornstarch mixture (slurry) to the boiling broth and stir until it thickens to the consistency of oil; add more of the slurry if necessary to achieve the correct consistency. Cool to room temperature before using.

Hush Puppies

1 quart corn oil

1 cup white cornmeal

5 cups flour

1 teaspoon baking powder

1 teaspoon salt

2 teaspoons sugar, or more to taste

¼ teaspoon freshly ground black pepper

Pinch of cayenne pepper

1 egg, beaten

½ cup milk

2 tablespoons butter, melted

¼ medium onion, minced

1 clove garlic, minced

In a deep-sided skillet, heat the oil over medium-high heat until it reaches 375°F. In a food processor, with a mixer, or by hand, mix the cornmeal, flour, baking powder, salt, sugar, pepper, and cayenne. In a bowl, blend the egg, milk, butter, onion, and garlic. Pour the egg mixture into the flour mixture and blend until a stiff batter forms. Drop heaping teaspoons of the batter into the heated oil and fry until golden brown. Remove the hush puppies from the oil and drain on paper towels. Keep warm in a low oven until ready to serve.

California Sunrise Salad with Sour Cream-Cilantro Dressing

This salad gets its name from the unique way of assembling the ingredients, which resemble a California sun in all its glory. The salad makes a good addition to a buffet, where guests can view the dramatic presentation.

Vegetable oil

Four 6-inch yellow corn tortillas cut into ⅛- by 2-inch strips

Salt to taste

SOUR CREAM-CILANTRO DRESSING

1 cup sour cream

½ cup mayonnaise

2 tablespoons malt vinegar

1 teaspoon Worcestershire sauce

1 tablespoon brown sugar

¼ cup chopped fresh cilantro

6 small heads baby romaine lettuce, leaves separated

1 to 2 heads radicchio, shaved very thinly crosswise

1 pint grape tomatoes or small cherry tomatoes

⅔ cup oil-cured olives

1 cup coarsely grated Monterey Jack cheese

FRY THE TORTILLAS | Heat 1 inch of oil in a deep-sided skillet over medium-high heat. In batches, fry the tortilla strips until very crisp. Drain on paper towels. Season with salt while still hot.

PREPARE THE DRESSING | In a bowl, mix together the sour cream, mayonnaise, vinegar, Worcestershire, brown sugar, and cilantro. Cover the bowl and refrigerate until needed.

ASSEMBLE THE SALAD | Place the romaine leaves in a bowl and toss with the dressing. Arrange the romaine neatly in the center of a large plate to resemble a sun. Sprinkle the shaved radicchio over the top. Place the grape tomatoes and olives in the center of the romaine and radicchio arrangement. Sprinkle the salad with the cheese and surround the salad with a wreath of the fried corn tortillas.

SERVES 4

Steamed Red Potatoes with Dulse and Ginger

Steamed red potatoes are perked up with the lively flavors of fresh ginger, green onions, and dulse. Steaming the potatoes with chicken broth adds another dimension of flavor.

2 cups chicken broth or water

6 to 8 thin slices fresh ginger

1 cup loose dulse leaves (see Chef's Tip)

12 small red potatoes (1 to 1¼ inches in diameter)

3 tablespoons unsalted butter

4 green onions, cut on the bias into ⅛-inch-thick slices

Salt and freshly ground black pepper to taste

2 tablespoons chopped or julienned dulse for garnish

COOK THE DULSE AND POTATOES | In the bottom of a steamer, put the broth or water, ginger, and dulse. Cover and simmer for 5 minutes. Place the potatoes in the top of the steamer and position it over the bottom of the steamer. Cover the steamer and cook until the potatoes are tender, about 25 to 30 minutes.

SAUTÉ THE GREEN ONIONS | In a large skillet, melt the butter over medium heat until it browns and smells nutty. Add the green onions and sauté for 30 seconds. Add the hot potatoes and dulse from the steamer and toss until coated with the butter and onions. Taste and season with salt and pepper.

GARNISH AND SERVE THE DISH | Transfer the potato mixture to a warm dish and sprinkle with the chopped or julienned dulse. Serve immediately.

SERVES 2 TO 3

➤ **CHEF'S TIP**

With its briny flavor, it is easy to guess dulse's origin—the ocean. It is actually a type of seaweed that comes from the seas around Britain. Red in color, look for dulse in an Asian market or health food store.

Potato, Onion, and Rosemary Pizza

For a snack or light luncheon entrée accompanied by a salad, this pizza, topped with an intriguing combination of potato, onion, and rosemary, is a perfect choice.

4 russet potatoes

¼ cup extra-virgin olive oil

¼ cup chopped fresh rosemary

2 tablespoons butter

2 medium onions, sliced

Pizza Dough (recipe follows)

½ teaspoon salt

¼ teaspoon freshly ground black pepper

COOK THE POTATOES | Peel the potatoes and cut them into smaller, even pieces. Place the potatoes in a bowl and combine with the olive oil and rosemary; toss well.

SAUTÉ THE ONIONS | In a skillet, melt the butter over medium-high heat. Add the onions and sauté until lightly golden brown; set aside.

SHAPE AND BAKE THE PIZZAS | Preheat the oven to 400°F, with a pizza stone, if desired. Divide the dough into 4 equal pieces. On a lightly floured work surface, roll out each piece of dough to a 6-inch disk. Top the dough with the potatoes and onions, dividing evenly, and season with salt and pepper. Transfer the pizzas to a baking sheet or the pizza stone. Bake the pizzas for 15 to 20 minutes, or until the crust is cooked through and golden brown on the edges.

SERVES 4

Pizza Dough

½ cup lukewarm water

1 tablespoon active dry yeast

1½ cups spring water

4 to 4½ cups all-purpose flour

3 tablespoons olive oil

1 to 2 teaspoons sea salt

Place the lukewarm water in a bowl. Add the yeast and let stand until puffy, about 10 minutes. Add the water, 4 cups of the flour, the olive oil, and salt and mix well in a food processor, with a mixer, or by hand. Adjust the consistency with more flour, if needed, and knead until the it is smooth and satiny.

Shape the dough into a ball and place it into a lightly oiled bowl. Cover the bowl with plastic wrap and let the dough rise in a draft-free location until doubled in size, about 1½ hours. Punch down the dough and shape and bake according to the desired recipe.

MAKES FOUR 6-INCH PIZZA CRUSTS

Grilled Vegetable Pizza with Fontina Cheese and Roasted Garlic

Though originating in Naples, Italy, pizza has become a quintessential American dish. In this country we are not shy about improvising the toppings—pizza shows up here in a multitude of guises.

1 bulb garlic

8 spears asparagus, tough ends trimmed

1 red bell pepper, halved and seeded

12 small white mushrooms, trimmed, quartered, and threaded on skewers

2 tablespoons extra-virgin olive oil

½ teaspoon salt

¼ teaspoon freshly ground black pepper

Pinch dried thyme

Pizza Dough (see page 59)

⅔ cup grated fontina cheese

1 teaspoon chopped fresh Italian parsley

1 teaspoon chopped fresh tarragon

1 teaspoon chopped fresh chives

ROAST THE GARLIC | Preheat the oven to 350°F. Wrap the garlic bulb with aluminum foil. Place the garlic in the oven and bake for about 45 minutes, until soft. Remove the foil and cool the bulb slightly. Peel the cloves and set aside.

GRILL THE VEGETABLES | Preheat the grill to medium-high (see page 41). Place the asparagus, peppers, and mushrooms in a roasting pan. Add the olive oil, salt, pepper, and thyme, and turn to coat the vegetables well with the oil and seasonings. Place the vegetables on the grill and cook, turning, until tender, about 6 to 8 minutes for the asparagus, 5 to 7 minutes for the peppers and mushrooms. Remove the mushrooms from the skewers and cut all of the vegetables into bite-sized pieces.

SHAPE AND BAKE THE PIZZAS | Increase the oven heat to 425°F, with a pizza stone, if desired. Divide the Pizza Dough into 10 equal pieces. On a lightly floured work surface, roll out each piece of dough to a 6-inch disk. Top the pizzas with the vegetables, garlic cloves, and fontina cheese, dividing evenly. Transfer the pizzas to a baking sheet or the pizza stone. Bake the pizzas for 15 to 20 minutes, or until the crust is cooked through and golden brown on the edges, and the cheese is melted.

GARNISH AND SERVE THE PIZZAS | Sprinkle the grilled pizzas with the fresh herbs and cut into wedges to serve.

SERVES 4

Sweet Pepper, Corn, and Chicken Pizza

Easy to put together, this brightly colored pizza uses barbecue sauce rather than tomato sauce as its base. It's a low-fat pizza, utilizing fresh vegetables and herbs, rather than cheese, to flavor it.

1 ear fresh corn

1 tablespoon olive oil

1½ cups homemade or purchased barbecue sauce

¾ pound chicken legs, skin removed

½ cup small diced onion

1 green bell pepper, cut into small dice

1 teaspoon chopped fresh sage

½ teaspoon salt

⅛ teaspoon freshly ground black pepper

Pizza Dough (see page 59)

GRILL THE CORN | Preheat the grill to medium high (see page 41). Place the corn, in its husk, on the grill and cook, turning, for 15 to 20 minutes; cool. When the corn is cool enough to handle, remove the husk and silk from the corn and cut the kernels from the cobs (see Chef's Tip).

GRILL THE CHICKEN | Place ¾ cup of the barbecue sauce in a cup or bowl for basting; reserve the remaining sauce separately. Place the chicken legs on the grill and cook, turning, for about 20 minutes, basting frequently with the basting sauce. When done, the chicken should have an internal temperature of 180°F. Remove the chicken from the grill. When cool enough to handle, remove the chicken meat from the bone and pull it with your fingers into coarse shreds.

SAUTÉ THE VEGETABLES | In a large skillet, heat the oil over medium heat. Add the onion and pepper and sauté for 4 to 5 minutes. Stir in the corn, sage, salt, and pepper, and set aside.

SHAPE AND BAKE THE PIZZAS | Preheat the oven to 400°F, with a pizza stone, if desired. Divide the dough into 10 equal pieces. On a lightly floured work surface, roll out each piece of dough to a 6-inch disk. Top the pizzas with the reserved barbecue sauce, the chicken, and the corn-pepper mixture, dividing evenly. Transfer the pizzas to a baking sheet, or the pizza stone. Bake the pizzas for 15 to 18 minutes, or until the crust is cooked through and golden brown on the edges.

SERVES 4

➤ **CHEF'S TIP**

To remove corn kernels from their cobs, snap or cut them in half. Stand each half up on a cutting board on its flat end. With a sharp knife, cut down the length of the cob on all sides to release the kernels.

Roasted Chicken Pot Pie with Cornbread Topping

For this new twist on chicken pot pie, cornbread forms the topping rather than a pastry crust. The next time you have a roasted chicken dinner, make an additional chicken and extra gravy and create this savory pie with the leftovers.

1¼ cups yellow cornmeal

1½ cups all-purpose flour

2 tablespoons sugar

1 teaspoon salt

2 tablespoons baking powder

2 eggs

1½ tablespoons butter, melted

1¼ to 1½ cups milk

One 3-pound chicken, roasted, warmed

½ cup fresh corn kernels, roasted

½ cup cooked, sliced okra

½ cup diced fresh tomato

½ cup cooked black-eyed peas

3 to 4 cups homemade or purchased chicken gravy (or as needed), heated

PREPARE THE CORNBREAD BATTER | Preheat the oven to 375°F. In a food processor, with a blender, or by hand, mix the cornmeal, flour, sugar, salt, baking powder, eggs, melted butter, and milk until a smooth batter forms.

ASSEMBLE THE POT PIE | Cut the drumsticks away from the chicken, and pull the breast and thigh meat from the bone in fairly large pieces. Place the chicken pieces in an ovenproof casserole. Distribute the corn, okra, tomato, and peas evenly over the chicken. Pour in the hot chicken gravy so that the ingredients are just covered. Top with the cornbread batter and spread evenly.

BAKE AND SERVE THE POT PIE | Place the pot pie in the oven and bake it until the cornbread is golden brown and the ingredients are heated through, about 45 to 60 minutes. Serve immediately.

SERVES 4

Red Chile-Seared Scallops with Jalapeño Grits

Two types of chiles enliven this dish, featuring sea scallops from the coast, grits from the southern states, and tequila from south of the border. Tomato salsa and tequila-lime sour cream are the accents.

½ pound yellow tomatoes, diced

½ pound red tomatoes, diced

1 medium onion, diced

3 cloves garlic, minced

3 jalapeño chiles, minced

3 tablespoons chopped fresh cilantro

¼ cup plus 1 teaspoon fresh lime juice

½ cup tomato juice

Salt to taste

¼ cup sour cream

2 tablespoons tequila

3 cups milk

2½ teaspoons salt

1½ cups grits

¼ cup ancho chile powder

2 teaspoons ground coriander

2 teaspoons confectioners' sugar

1 teaspoon chili powder

1 teaspoon ground cumin

1 teaspoon dried thyme

2 pounds sea scallops, side muscle removed

3 tablespoons olive oil

MAKE THE TOMATO SALSA | In a glass or stainless steel bowl, mix together the red and yellow tomatoes, the onion, garlic, two-thirds of the jalapeños, the cilantro, ¼ cup of the lime juice, the tomato juice, and salt to taste. Set aside. To make a more finely textured salsa, combine the ingredients in a food processor and pulse until the desired texture is reached.

MAKE THE TEQUILA-LIME SOUR CREAM | In another glass or stainless steel bowl, mix together the sour cream, tequila, the remaining 1 teaspoon lime juice, and salt to taste. Set aside.

MAKE THE GRITS | In a saucepan, combine the milk, ½ teaspoon of the salt, and the grits and bring to a boil over high heat. Reduce the heat to low and simmer slowly for 10 minutes. Stir in the remaining jalapeño, and season with salt to taste; keep warm.

SEASON THE SCALLOPS | Preheat the oven to 400°F. In a shallow dish, mix together the ancho chile powder, coriander, confectioner's sugar, the remaining 2 teaspoons salt, the chili powder, cumin, and thyme. Add the scallops to the dish and toss well to coat with the mixture.

COOK THE SCALLOPS | In a large ovenproof skillet, heat the olive oil over medium-high heat until smoking. Add the scallops and sear them on both sides. Place the skillet in the oven and cook the scallops for about 3 to 4 minutes, until firm and opaque.

GARNISH AND SERVE THE DISH | Divide the scallops among 6 serving plates accompanied by the grits, the tomato salsa, and the tequila-lime sour cream.

SERVES 6

Ribs Southwestern Style

Utilize purchased barbecue sauce as the base for the zippy southwestern-style sauce that coats pork spareribs. Smoky chipotle chiles, orange juice, orange marmalade, and lots of spices add intriguing flavor to the mix.

4 pounds pork spareribs

Salt and freshly ground black pepper to taste

1 tablespoon cumin seeds, toasted and pulverized with an electric coffee mill

2 cups prepared barbecue sauce

1 cup orange juice

¼ cup orange marmalade

2 chipotle chiles in adobo (see Chef's Tip, page 27)

½ teaspoon ground cinnamon

½ teaspoon ground cumin

¼ teaspoon ground allspice

¼ cup cider or red wine vinegar

⅛ teaspoon ground cloves

½ teaspoon salt

Green onions, sliced on the diagonal, for garnish

PREBAKE THE RIBS | Preheat the oven to 325°F. Place the ribs on racks on rimmed baking sheets. Sprinkle the ribs with salt, pepper, and the toasted cumin. Place the ribs in the oven and bake for about 1½ hours.

MAKE THE BARBECUE SAUCE | In a saucepan, combine the prepared barbecue sauce, orange juice, marmalade, chipotles, cinnamon, ground cumin, allspice, vinegar, cloves, and salt. Bring the mixture to a simmer. Pour a small amount of sauce into another bowl for basting; set the remaining sauce aside.

GRILL AND SERVE THE RIBS | Build a medium-hot barbecue fire or preheat a gas grill to medium (see page 41). Place the partially cooked spareribs on the grill and cook, turning frequently, for about 40 to 45 minutes, until the meat is fork tender and reaches an internal temperature of 170°F. During the last 20 minutes of cooking, brush the ribs with the basting sauce. Remove the ribs from the grill and let them rest briefly before serving. Transfer the ribs to a serving platter and sprinkle with green onions. Pass the remaining barbecue sauce at the table.

SERVES 4

Albuquerque Grilled Pork with Beans and Greens Sauté

Chef Heywood prepared this dish by threading the scored pork tenderloin on a curved skewer to create a fan shape. Though not as dramatic, it's every bit as delicious grilled and served in its natural state.

3 tablespoons chili powder

2 teaspoons onion powder

1 teaspoon garlic powder

½ teaspoon ground cumin

½ teaspoon ground Mexican oregano

½ teaspoon ground coriander

½ teaspoon freshly ground black pepper

One pork tenderloin, about 1 pound, trimmed

Olive oil

2 tablespoons concentrated pomegranate juice (see Chef's Tip)

1 tablespoon molasses

1 tablespoon sherry

Beans and Greens Sauté (recipe follows)

SPRINKLE THE PORK WITH THE DRY RUB | In a bowl, mix together the chili powder, onion powder, garlic powder, cumin, oregano, coriander, and pepper. With the point of a sharp knife, make crosswise cuts ¾-inch deep and ¾-inch long down the length of the pork tenderloin. Sprinkle the surface of the pork with the dry rub, avoiding the cuts and taking care not to use too much of the dry rub (you don't want to dredge it). Refrigerate the pork for 2 to 4 hours.

GRILL THE PORK | Preheat the grill to medium-low (see page 41). Thread the pork tenderloin onto a curved skewer, creating a fan shape (optional). Brush a very small amount of olive oil onto the pork. Grill the pork for 3 to 4 minutes on each side, to an internal temperature of 170°F.

PREPARE THE SAUCE | While the pork is grilling, mix together the pomegranate juice, molasses, and sherry.

SERVE THE PORK | When the pork is done, place it on a small platter and drizzle it with some of the sauce. Serve the pork immediately accompanied by the Beans and Greens Sauté.

SERVES 2

➤ **CHEF'S TIP**
Concentrated pomegranate juice is a common ingredient in North African and Middle Eastern cuisine. Look for it in a Middle Eastern or Moroccan market, or in a specialty food store.

Beans and Greens Sauté

2 tablespoons olive oil

2 cloves garlic, chopped

1 pound cleaned beet greens, coarsely chopped into 1-inch pieces

1 cup cooked or canned navy beans, warmed

1 cup cooked or canned black beans, warmed

½ cup chicken broth

Salt and freshly ground black pepper to taste

Malt vinegar to taste

In a large skillet, heat the olive oil over medium heat. Add the garlic and sauté until its aroma is apparent, taking care not to brown or scorch it. Add the beet greens and toss briskly with a wooden spoon. As the beet greens wilt and cook, add the warmed beans and the broth and toss until the ingredients are well mixed and heated through. Taste and season with salt, pepper, and vinegar.

Beef Tri Tip with Wild Mushroom Sauté

Tri tip is a triangular chunk of beef that comes from the sirloin. Any leftovers of this lean, tender meat can be used, thinly sliced for sandwiches or salads. An earthy mushroom sauté is a terrific partner.

2 ounces dried mushroom powder (see Chef's Tip)

1 teaspoon onion powder

1 teaspoon garlic powder

¼ teaspoon freshly ground black pepper

1 teaspoon dried thyme

¼ teaspoon ground cumin

1 teaspoon paprika

1 teaspoon salt

3½ pounds beef tri tip roast, tied (ask your butcher)

½ cup peanut oil

Wild Mushroom Sauté (recipe follows)

COAT THE BEEF WITH THE DRY RUB | In a bowl, mix together the mushroom powder, onion powder, garlic powder, pepper, thyme, cumin, paprika, and salt. Coat the beef on all sides with the mixture and place it on a plate. Cover and refrigerate the meat for 3 hours.

GRILL/ROAST THE MEAT | Preheat the grill to medium-low (see page 41). Brush the beef with peanut oil and place it on the grill. Cover the grill and cook the beef for 1 about hour, brushing frequently with peanut oil, until it reaches 145°F for medium-rare or 170°F for well-done. Remove the beef from the grill and let it stand for 7 to 10 minutes.

SLICE AND SERVE THE BEEF | Remove the strings from the beef and cut it into slices to serve. Serve with the Wild Mushroom Sauté.

SERVES 10

➤ **CHEF'S TIP**
Look for dried mushroom powder in a health food or specialty food store. Or, make your own by whirling dried mushrooms in an electric coffee mill.

Wild Mushroom Sauté

2 ½ pounds assorted wild and domestic mushrooms (see Chef's Tip)

¼ cup peanut oil

2 small shallots, minced

2 cloves garlic, minced

2 tablespoons butter

3 tablespoons chopped fresh Italian parsley

1 teaspoon salt

¼ teaspoon freshly ground black pepper

Wipe or brush the mushrooms to clean them. Trim the stem ends to just remove the brown ends. Depending on the shape of the mushroom, or the individual preference, slice, halve, quarter, or leave the mushrooms whole; try to keep the mushroom pieces the same size to ensure even cooking.

In a large skillet, heat the oil over high heat until smoking. Add the mushrooms, shallots, and garlic and sauté quickly for 3 to 5 minutes. Add the butter, parsley, salt, and pepper and mix thoroughly. Serve warm.

► CHEF'S TIP

Most of the "wild" mushrooms found in stores today are not really foraged from the woods, but are cultivated by producers. For this recipe, choose a mixture of different types of mushrooms, such as oyster, chanterelle, cremini (brown), white, and/or shiitake (be sure to stem the shiitakes).

Mexican Chocolate Cake with Caramel Whipped Cream

The caramel whipped cream is made using a traditional Mexican method of boiling condensed milk in the can until it is thick and naturally caramelized. Called "cajeta" in Mexico, the rich paste that results is usually made from goats milk.

1½ cups heavy cream

6 ounces Mexican chocolate, chopped (see Chef's Tip)

1 teaspoon ground cinnamon

One 13½-ounce can sweetened condensed milk

1 cup heavy cream, whipped

1 teaspoon ground cinnamon

10 tablespoons butter

5½ ounces Mexican chocolate, chopped

3 eggs

3 egg yolks

¼ cup sugar

½ cup cake flour, sifted

¼ ounce Mexican chocolate, grated

2 teaspoons vanilla extract

Confectioners' sugar for garnish

➤ CHEF'S TIP
Mexican chocolate is flavored with sugar, cinnamon, and ground almonds, and has a much grainier texture than regular chocolate. Look for it in a Latin American market or good grocery store.

PREPARE THE CHOCOLATE GANACHE | In a heavy bottomed stainless steel saucepan, bring the 1½ cups heavy cream to a boil over medium heat. Stir in the 6 ounces Mexican chocolate and 1 teaspoon of the cinnamon and blend well until the chocolate melts. Chill the mixture until firm.

MAKE THE CARAMEL WHIPPED CREAM | Place the can of milk in a heavy-bottomed stainless steel saucepan. Fill the pan with water and bring to a boil over high heat. Continue to boil gently for 1½ hours, adding more water if necessary. Remove the milk from the water and cool completely in the can. When cool, pour the milk into a bowl with the whipped cream and the remaining 1 teaspoon cinnamon. Whisk together well and chill until ready to serve.

PREPARE THE CAKE BATTER | Preheat the oven to 375°F. Butter twelve 4-ounce ramekins, completely coating the sides. In a heavy-bottomed stainless steel saucepan, melt the 10 tablespoons butter. Remove from the heat, add the 5½ ounces Mexican chocolate, and stir until it is completely melted; set aside. Whip the eggs, egg yolks and sugar with a mixer or by hand until they are a light lemon color and tripled in volume. With a rubber spatula, carefully fold in the sifted flour and the chocolate-butter mixture. Whip with a mixer on medium speed or by hand until the mixture is light and glossy. With the spatula, fold in the grated chocolate and vanilla extract.

FILL THE RAMEKINS AND BAKE THE CAKES | Transfer the cake batter to a pastry bag with no tip. Using the pastry bag, fill the prepared ramekins ¾ full. With a ½-ounce scoop or small spoon, place a small portion of the prepared ganache into the center of each filled ramekin. Bake the cakes for approximately 8 to 10 minutes. The cakes should be firm around the edges and pull away from the sides slightly. The finished cakes will be completely cooked on the outside, but soft on the inside.

GARNISH AND SERVE THE CAKES | As soon as the cakes come out of the oven, unmold them and transfer them to serving plates. Dust the cakes with confectioners' sugar and garnish with dollops of the caramel whipped cream.

SERVES 12

Kentucky Bourbon Black Bottom Pie

> Rather than with rum, this layered chocolate and custard tart is flavored with Kentucky bourbon, making it a true Southern treat. A thick layer of chocolate "ganache" on the bottom gives the pie its name.

FILLING BASE

¾ cup heavy cream

¾ cup milk

9 tablespoons sugar

½ vanilla bean

3 egg yolks

4 teaspoons cornstarch

4 teaspoons gelatin

3 tablespoons bourbon

1 teaspoon vanilla extract

3 ounces chocolate, chopped, melted

Tart Dough, baked (see page 163)

3 egg whites

¼ cup sugar

2 cups heavy cream

Shaved chocolate for garnish (optional)

Confectioners' sugar for garnish (optional)

PREPARE THE FILLING BASE | In a heavy-bottomed stainless steel saucepan, combine the heavy cream, ½ cup of the milk, 3 tablespoons of the sugar, and the vanilla bean. Bring the mixture to a boil over high heat. Meanwhile, in a stainless steel bowl, whisk together the egg yolks, the remaining 3 tablespoons sugar, and the cornstarch. When the milk mixture comes to a boil, whisk one cup of it into the egg yolk mixture and whisk well. Then, whisk the hot yolk mixture into the milk mixture on the stove, and bring it just to a boil. Set the mixture aside.

SOFTEN THE GELATIN | In the top of a double boiler or stainless steel bowl, over gently boiling water, combine the remaining ¼ cup milk with the gelatin, stirring to distribute the gelatin. Let the mixture stand for 2 to 3 minutes. Stir into the hot filling base until the gelatin is completely dissolved. Add the bourbon and vanilla. Reserve 1 cup of this mixture. Cool the remainder until it mounds slightly when dropped from a spoon.

PREPARE THE CHOCOLATE LAYER | Add the cup of reserved hot filling base to the bowl with the melted chocolate and mix well. Pour the chocolate mixture into the cooled tart shell, spreading it evenly. Place in the freezer for 15 minutes.

LIGHTEN THE FILLING BASE WITH EGG WHITES | In a clean, oil-free bowl, whip the egg whites with mixer or by hand until foamy. Add the remaining 3 tablespoons sugar and whip until medium peaks form. Gently fold the egg whites into the filling base. Spread the filling over the chocolate layer of the tart and place in the refrigerator until set.

GARNISH AND SERVE THE TART | At serving time, whip the 2 cups heavy cream with a mixer or by hand until medium-stiff peaks form. Spread the whipped cream decoratively over the pie and cut into wedges. Alternatively, pipe whipped cream rosettes onto individual wedges of the pie. Garnish portions with chocolate shavings and/or confectioners' sugar, if desired.

MAKES ONE 10-INCH TART; SERVES 10 TO 12

Upside-Down Dutch Apple Cake

This rustic skillet cake takes few ingredients and is easy to prepare. You can put it together just before eating your main course and it will be ready to serve warm at dessert time. Vanilla ice cream is a lovely companion.

6 baking apples, peeled

Cinnamon sugar to taste (see Chef's Tip)

1 cup all-purpose flour

¾ cup sugar

2 eggs

½ cup butter, melted

1 teaspoon vanilla extract

PREPARE THE APPLES | Preheat the oven to 375°F. Cut the apples into wedges and arrange them in the bottom of a well-buttered 10-inch cast-iron skillet. Sprinkle the apples with cinnamon sugar.

MAKE THE CAKE BATTER | In a bowl, with a mixer or by hand, combine the flour and sugar. Add the eggs, butter, and vanilla to the flour mixture and mix until a smooth batter forms. Pour the batter evenly over the apples.

BAKE AND SERVE THE CAKE | Bake the cake for 45 minutes, or until the batter is cooked through and browned on top. Remove the pan from the oven and cool the cake for 30 minutes. Invert the cake onto a serving plate. Cut into wedges and serve warm.

MAKES ONE 10-INCH CAKE; SERVES 8

➤ CHEF'S TIP

Cinnamon sugar is good to have on hand and easy to make. Stir 1½ teaspoons ground cinnamon into 1 cup sugar. Adjust the amount of cinnamon to suit your taste.

California Fruit Slice with Whipped Cream

Here's a fresh take on fruit tart, boasting a sponge cake base rather than a pastry crust. Choose your favorite types of seasonal fruits for the topping, preferably from your local farmers' market or roadside farmstand. Serve it with fresh berry sauce, if desired.

SPONGE CAKE

5 eggs

3 egg yolks

7 tablespoons sugar

1½ teaspoons vanilla extract

1 cup cake flour, sifted twice

FILLING

1¼ cups heavy cream

3 tablespoons Grand Marnier

6 tablespoons confectioners' sugar

Grated zest of 1 orange

1½ tablespoons water

1½ teaspoons gelatin

SIMPLE SYRUP

½ cup water

½ cup granulated sugar

2 tablespoons Grand Marnier

1 cup apricot jam

Sliced seasonal fruits and berries

Whipped cream for garnish

MAKE THE SPONGE CAKE | Preheat the oven to 425°F. In a stainless steel bowl, combine the eggs, egg yolks, and sugar. Place the bowl over a saucepan that contains a small amount of simmering water and whisk constantly until the mixture reaches 120°F. Whip with a mixer or by hand until the mixture is very full in volume and recedes slightly from the highest point that it reached in the bowl. With a rubber spatula, carefully fold in 1 teaspoon of the vanilla extract and the sifted flour. Spread the batter evenly onto a level 15- by 10-inch parchment-lined rimmed baking sheet. Bake until golden brown, about 7 to 8 minutes. Cool the cake completely, wrap with plastic wrap, and reserve.

PREPARE THE FILLING | With a mixer or by hand, whip the heavy cream until soft peaks form. Fold in the Grand Marnier, confectioners' sugar, orange zest, and the remaining ½ teaspoon of the vanilla. In another bowl, combine the water and gelatin and let stand for 2 to 3 minutes. Place over a saucepan of simmering water and stir until the gelatin is completely melted. Quickly blend the gelatin mixture into the flavored whipped cream.

PREPARE THE SIMPLE SYRUP | In a saucepan, combine the water and granulated sugar. Heat until the sugar is dissolved. Cool and add the Grand Marnier.

ASSEMBLE THE BASE | Cut the sponge cake in half lengthwise and place one half browned-side up on a baking sheet. Brush the cake lightly with the simple syrup and spread the flavored whipped cream evenly over the top. Carefully place the remaining half of the cake, browned-side down, on top of the whipped cream, making sure that it is level. Carefully wrap the filled cake with plastic wrap and refrigerate or freeze until needed.

GARNISH AND SERVE THE CAKE | In a small saucepan, bring the jam to a boil and stir until smooth, thinning with a small amount of water. Strain the glaze and spread an even layer on top of the well-chilled cake (thaw the cake if frozen). Arrange slices of fruits and berries on top in a decorative manner and brush the fruit with the hot glaze. Chill the dessert briefly. With a warm knife, cut the dessert into serving pieces. Serve with fresh whipped cream.

SERVES 20

Italian

cuisine is one of the most popular types of food today. Just look in any bookstore's cookbook section and you'll find a multitude of volumes on every conceivable regional Italian cooking style and cooking technique.

One thing that all regions of Italy have in common is their insistence on top-quality, regionally produced raw ingredients for their recipes, whether in the finest dining establishments, humble village trattorias, or country villas.

This chapter offers several recipes typical of the foods you would eat in Rome, Tuscany, and Sicily.

Braised Artichokes in Lemon and Herbs Sauce

This makes a light, tangy appetizer early in artichoke season—March through May—when the tiny artichokes have not yet formed their hairy "chokes" and taste of the essence of spring.

1 cup water

3 cloves garlic, peeled and left whole

5 to 6 parsley stems

5 to 6 basil stems

Juice of 1 lemon

12 baby artichokes

2 tablespoons olive oil

½ cup chopped fresh Italian parsley

½ cup chopped fresh basil leaves

¼ cup dry bread crumbs

2 tablespoons freshly grated Parmesan cheese

Salt and freshly ground black pepper to taste

MAKE THE BRAISING LIQUID | In a saucepan, combine the water, garlic, parsley stems, basil stems, and lemon juice and bring to a simmer over medium-high heat; simmer for 5 minutes. Strain the mixture, reserving the liquid and solids separately.

PREPARE AND BRAISE THE ARTICHOKES | Preheat the oven to 375°F. With a knife, trim the artichoke stems and remove any sharp barbs from the leaves. Cut the artichokes in half lengthwise and remove the choke if it has started to form. Place the artichokes in a baking dish and toss them with the olive oil until they are evenly coated. Add the chopped parsley, basil, reserved garlic cloves, bread crumbs, and Parmesan. Stir in half of the braising liquid. Cover the baking dish tightly, place it in the oven, and cook the artichokes for 30 minutes. With a slotted spoon, transfer the artichokes to a platter.

MAKE THE SAUCE AND SERVE | Transfer the remaining contents of the baking pan to a blender and process until it forms a paste. Add a small amount of the remaining braising liquid to make a thick sauce. Taste the sauce and season with salt and pepper. Pour the sauce over the artichokes and serve warm or at room temperature.

SERVES 12 AS AN APPETIZER

Insalata Pantesca | Potato Salad with Tomatoes and Olives

Make this salad in the late summer when tomatoes are at the peak of their season and are available in a variety of colors. Be sure to taste the salad before seasoning it; the olives will provide quite a bit of salt to the mixture.

12 medium-sized red potatoes, scrubbed

2 yellow tomatoes, seeded and cut into medium dice

2 red tomatoes, seeded and cut into medium dice

1 red onion, thinly sliced lengthwise

½ cup pitted oil-cured olives

1 tablespoon drained capers

2 teaspoons dried oregano

¼ cup olive oil, or to taste

Salt and freshly ground black pepper to taste

COOK AND SLICE THE POTATOES | Cook the potatoes in a pan of simmering salted water until tender enough to pierce easily with the tip of a paring knife, about 25 to 40 minutes, depending upon the size of the potatoes. Drain the potatoes and return them to the pan. Place the pan over low heat, shaking the pan frequently, until the steam has been driven off the potatoes. Transfer the potatoes to a shallow dish and let them stand until just cool enough to handle. Slice the potatoes and place them in a salad bowl.

TOSS THE SALAD INGREDIENTS | Add the tomatoes, onion, olives, capers, and oregano to the bowl. Add the olive oil and toss gently to combine the ingredients, taking care that the potatoes don't break apart. Taste the salad and season with salt and pepper. The salad can be prepared up to 24 hours in advance; refrigerate it until ready to serve. Serve the salad at room temperature.

SERVES 6 AS A SIDE DISH

Cozze Ripieno | Stuffed Mussels

For lively color, you can use a combination of different colors of roasted peppers in place of the standard red. For a dramatic, restaurant-style presentation, serve the mussels on a bed of rock salt.

⅓ cup plus 2 tablespoons extra-virgin olive oil

2 tablespoons finely diced onion

2 tablespoons finely diced zucchini

2 tablespoons finely diced pepperoncini

6 tablespoons finely diced roasted red bell peppers

2 tablespoons red wine vinegar

1 tablespoon minced fresh Italian parsley

Salt and freshly ground black pepper to taste

¼ cup minced onion

1 cup fish stock, bottled clam juice, or water

1 bay leaf

36 mussels, thoroughly scrubbed and debearded (see Chef's Tip)

SAUTÉ THE VEGETABLES FOR THE FILLING | In a skillet, heat 2 tablespoons of the olive oil over medium-high heat. Add the finely diced onion, zucchini, and pepperoncini and sauté until the vegetables are tender, about 8 to 10 minutes. Transfer the vegetables to a bowl and stir in the roasted peppers. Refrigerate the mixture until it is very cold.

MAKE THE VINAIGRETTE | In a bowl, whisk together the remaining ⅓ cup oil, the vinegar, parsley, salt, and pepper, until blended.

STEAM THE MUSSELS | In a deep pot, combine the minced onion, stock, and bay leaf and bring to a simmer over medium heat. Add the mussels, cover the pot tightly, and steam them for about 6 to 8 minutes, or until the shells are opened. Discard any mussels that do not open. Pull away and discard the top shells of each mussel, and cool the mussels to room temperature.

FILL AND SERVE THE MUSSELS | Spoon a small amount of the vegetable stuffing on top of each mussel and arrange them on a platter. Whisk the dressing and drizzle it over the mussels. Keep the stuffed mussels refrigerated until ready to serve.

SERVES 6 AS AN APPETIZER

➤ CHEF'S TIP
Occasionally you may find hairy filaments attached to the side of the mussel shells called "beards." Pull off the beards with your fingers and scrub the mussels well under running water before cooking.

Mozzarella in Carrozza
Mozzarella in a Carriage

A grilled cheese in the Italian style, slices of mozzarella are sandwiched between slices of hearty bread, dipped in an egg-cheese batter and fried until golden brown. Add a tossed green salad for a quick lunchtime meal.

3 eggs

¼ cup freshly grated Romano cheese

Salt and freshly ground black pepper to taste

8 slices French-style bread

1 pound mozzarella cheese, thinly sliced

¾ cup olive oil

Fresh Tomato Sauce (see page 15) *or sliced tomatoes* (optional)

Thin lemon slices (optional)

MAKE THE BATTER | In a shallow bowl or glass pie plate, mix the eggs, Romano cheese, salt, and pepper.

ASSEMBLE THE SANDWICHES | Place 4 slices of the bread on a work surface. Place the mozzarella on top of the bread, dividing evenly, and top with the remaining 4 slices of the bread.

COAT AND COOK THE SANDWICHES | In a large skillet, heat the oil over medium-high heat. When the oil is hot, dip the sandwiches in the egg mixture until they are coated. Place the sandwiches in the pan and cook for 2 minutes on each side, or until golden brown. Adjust the heat if necessary to avoid burning the sandwiches. Drain the cooked sandwiches briefly on paper towels.

GARNISH AND SERVE THE SANDWICHES | Serve the sandwiches immediately with the Fresh Tomato Sauce or tomato slices, or with thin slices of lemon.

MAKES 4 SANDWICHES

Fagioli e Salsicce | Beans and Sausage

White beans are a common ingredient in many regional Italian cuisines. Here they pair with Italian sausage, tomatoes, and herbs for a pleasing first course for an Italian-themed dinner.

½ pound dried cannellini beans, soaked overnight in water to cover by 3 inches

½ onion, cut into small dice

3 cloves garlic, peeled and left whole

½ bunch plus 6 fresh sage leaves

1 teaspoon salt, or to taste

6 tablespoons olive oil

6 links sweet Italian sausage

3 teaspoons minced garlic

2 cups chicken broth

6 plum tomatoes, seeded, drained, and chopped

Salt and freshly ground black pepper to taste

COOK THE BEANS | Drain the beans, rinse them, and transfer them to a pot. Add the onion, garlic, half-bunch of sage, and enough cold water to cover the beans by 1 inch. Bring the water to a simmer over low heat and cook for 1 to 1½ hours, or until the beans are tender. Add the salt and continue to simmer for another 10 minutes. Drain the beans and set aside.

SAUTÉ THE SAUSAGE AND THE FLAVORINGS | In a large skillet, heat the oil over medium heat. Add the sausage and sauté until most of the pink color is gone. Add the garlic and sauté for 1 minute. Add the broth, tomatoes, and 6 sage leaves and simmer over low heat, stirring occasionally, until the sausage is cooked through, about 15 minutes.

COMBINE THE INGREDIENTS AND SERVE | Add the drained beans to the skillet and simmer until the beans are heated through. Taste and season with salt and pepper. Serve in heated soup plates or bowls.

SERVES 6 AS A FIRST COURSE

Pasta all'Amatriciana
Amatrice-Style Pasta

Cooked in the style of Amatrice, in the Lazio province of Italy, this pasta dish is sauced with a spicy combination of tomatoes, bacon, and wine. It makes a great weeknight meal, as many ingredients are probably already on hand.

3 teaspoons olive oil

1 cup finely chopped onion

6 ounces pancetta or bacon, chopped (see Chef's Tips)

1 teaspoon finely chopped garlic

½ cup dry white wine

One 28-ounce can whole plum tomatoes with juice, finely chopped

1 teaspoon seeded, finely chopped serrano chile pepper, or ¼ teaspoon red pepper flakes

Salt to taste

1 pound bucatini or perciatelli pasta (see Chef's Tips)

⅔ cup freshly grated Romano cheese, plus more for passing

1 tablespoon chopped fresh basil leaves (optional)

COOK THE SAUCE | In a large skillet, heat the oil over medium heat. Add the onion and sauté until golden brown. Add the pancetta or bacon, and garlic and sauté for about 5 minutes. Add the wine and cook until it evaporates. Add the tomatoes and their juice, the chile pepper or pepper flakes, and the salt. Simmer for about 30 minutes.

COOK THE PASTA | In a large pot of boiling salted water, cook the pasta according to the directions on the package until slightly firm to the bite, *al dente*. Drain the pasta and place it in a large serving dish.

MIX THE PASTA WITH THE SAUCE AND SERVE | Add the sauce, cheese, and basil, if desired, to the dish and toss the ingredients until well mixed. Serve immediately. Pass additional grated cheese at the table.

SERVES 4

➤ CHEF'S TIPS

Pancetta is seasoned, cured Italian bacon. Look for it in an Italian deli or specialty food store. Bucatini and perciatelli are long, hollow pasta noodles. You can also use penne or another type of pasta that will catch the sauce in its crevices.

Timballo de Riso e Macaroni | Rice and Pasta Mold

In Italy, macaroni serves as a generic word for many different tubular shapes of pasta. Here ziti or penne combine with a meat, tomato, and vegetable sauce, and it is enclosed in a mold of Arborio rice. Reserve this dish for a special occasion.

2 pounds Arborio rice

5 eggs, beaten

2½ cups freshly grated Parmesan or locatelli cheese, plus more for garnish

¼ cup olive oil

½ cup minced onion

¼ pound cremini (brown) mushrooms, trimmed and sliced

1 pound ground turkey

2 tablespoons tomato paste

Two 28-ounce cans whole tomatoes, pureed with a food processor

Salt and freshly ground black pepper to taste

Sugar to taste

Freshly grated nutmeg to taste

Leaves from 3 sprigs fresh basil, minced

1 pound ziti or penne pasta

1 cup shelled fresh or frozen green peas

Dried bread crumbs

1 tablespoon milk

Quick Tomato Sauce (recipe follows)

COOK THE RICE | Bring a large pot of salted water to a rolling boil. Add the rice in a thin stream, stirring with a fork to prevent the rice from clumping. Simmer the rice over medium heat for 15 to 16 minutes, or until the rice is tender. Drain the rice through a fine mesh sieve. Spread the hot rice on a baking sheet in a thin layer to cool it quickly.

MAKE AND CHILL THE RICE MIXTURE | When the rice has cooled to room temperature, transfer it to a bowl. Add 4 of the eggs and 2 cups of the grated cheese. Stir the mixture well with a wooden spoon and place it in the refrigerator for several hours or overnight, until it is well chilled and firm.

MAKE THE FILLING | In a large saucepan, heat the olive oil over medium heat. Add the onion and sauté until golden, about 12 to 15 minutes. Increase the heat to medium-high and add the mushrooms. Sauté for about 6 to 8 minutes, or until the liquid that is released has cooked away. Add the ground turkey and sauté over medium heat until no pink remains. Add the tomato paste and sauté for 1 minute. Stir in the pureed tomatoes and bring the mixture to a simmer. Simmer until the filling has a good consistency and flavor, about 45 minutes. Taste the filling and season with salt, pepper, sugar, and nutmeg. Stir in the basil and remove the filling from the heat. Strain the filling through a colander, catching the liquid in a bowl and allowing the solids to remain in the colander.

COOK THE PASTA | While the filling is simmering, cook the pasta in a large pot of boiling salted water according to the package directions until slightly undercooked. Drain the pasta well and place it in a large bowl. Add a small amount of the strained filling liquid, using only enough to barely coat the pasta. Add the reserved filling solids, the peas, and the remaining ½ cup of the grated cheese and stir well.

(recipe continues on following page)

ASSEMBLE THE TIMBALE | Preheat the oven to 400°F. Brush a 5-quart ovenproof bowl with butter and coat it with bread crumbs. Press a generous three-fourths of the chilled rice mixture into the bowl, making a ½-inch-thick layer around the bowl. Fill the rice-lined bowl with the pasta mixture. Top the pasta mixture with the remaining rice mixture, spreading it in an even layer over the pasta. Seal the rim of the timbale well to enclose the filling. In a small bowl, beat the remaining egg with the milk. Brush the top of the timbale with the egg mixture.

BAKE THE TIMBALE | Place the timbale on the center oven rack. Bake for about 1 hour, or until the rice is rich golden brown. Remove the timbale from the oven and gently loosen it from the bowl using a small knife. Let the timbale stand for about 15 minutes.

UNMOLD THE TIMBALE AND SERVE | Invert the timbale onto a serving platter and cut it into wedges. Serve it with the Quick Tomato Sauce, grated cheese, and freshly ground black pepper.

SERVES 6 TO 8

Quick Tomato Sauce

One 28-ounce can whole tomatoes, chopped

Two 8-ounce cans tomato puree or sauce

2 tablespoons butter, sliced and chilled

Salt and freshly ground black pepper to taste

In a food processor, process the whole tomatoes until a coarse puree forms. Transfer the tomatoes to a saucepan and bring to a simmer. Add the tomato puree and continue to simmer for another 10 minutes. Scatter the sliced butter over the surface of the tomato sauce and swirl the pan until the butter is incorporated. Taste the sauce and season with salt and pepper.

Bistecca alla Fiorentina | Grilled T-Bone Steak, Tuscan Style

Be sure to use only the finest ingredients for this steak, grilled in the simple style of the region of Tuscany. Accompanied by fresh tomato bruschetta, this entrée can be served either as a weeknight meal or casual company dinner.

One T-bone steak, cut 2 inches thick

Salt and freshly ground black pepper to taste

¼ cup extra-virgin olive oil

Juice of 1 lemon

Bruschetta (recipe follows)

GRILL THE STEAK | Preheat a grill to high (see page 41). Grill the steak over direct heat (see page 24) for about 10 minutes on the first side. Turn the steak and finish cooking on the second side, another 10 to 12 minutes for rare, to an internal temperature of 135°F. (For medium doneness, increase the cooking time to 12 minutes per side, 145°F; for well-done, increase the cooking time to 15 minutes per side, 170°F.) Move the steak to a cooler area on the grill if necessary to avoid overcooking the exterior. Season the steak with salt and pepper just before removing it from the grill.

GARNISH AND SERVE THE STEAK | When the steak has reached the desired doneness, transfer it to a cutting board or large platter. Drizzle the steak with the olive oil and finish by sprinkling the steak with lemon juice. Cut the steak into serving portions and serve with Bruschetta.

SERVES 4

Bruschetta

One 8-ounce loaf Italian or French bread, cut into 8 slices

1 clove garlic, cut in half

½ cup olive oil

2 large, ripe tomatoes, cut into thick slices

Salt and freshly ground black pepper to taste

Fresh oregano leaves to taste (optional)

Preheat the oven to 350°F. Arrange the bread slices on a baking rack and bake them for about 8 to 10 minutes, until they are browned on both sides. Arrange the bread on a platter and rub the cut side of the garlic clove on one side of each slice. Drizzle about one tablespoon of olive oil over each slice of bread. Top the bread with the tomato slices, and sprinkle with salt, pepper, and fresh oregano, if desired. Serve immediately.

Saltimbocca alla Romana | Veal Scallops with Sage and Prosciutto

Saltimbocca, literally translated, means "jump in the mouth," alluding to the bold flavors present in the dish. Good companions to this recipe are risotto and sautéed broccoli rabe.

Eight 4-ounce veal scallops

4 large fresh sage leaves

8 thin slices prosciutto

½ cup instant flour, such as Wondra

Salt and freshly ground black pepper to taste

½ cup butter

¼ cup olive oil

1 cup veal stock or dry white wine

FILL AND POUND THE VEAL SCALLOPS | Lay one veal scallop on a work surface and top with one sage leaf and one slice of prosciutto. Place another veal scallop on top of the prosciutto. Place the "sandwich" on a piece of plastic wrap that is 4 times the size of the veal. Place an equal-sized piece of plastic wrap on top of the veal and pound it with a meat mallet to an even thickness. Continue the layering and pounding process with the remaining veal, prosciutto, and sage.

DREDGE AND SAUTÉ THE VEAL SCALLOPS | Place the flour in a shallow dish. Season the veal with salt and pepper and dredge it in the flour. In a large skillet, melt half of the butter with the olive oil over medium heat. Add the veal and gently sauté for approximately 4 minutes, turning once. Transfer the veal to a warm serving platter.

DEGLAZE THE PAN | Add the stock or white wine to the pan and stir to scrape up the browned bits. When the liquid is slightly reduced, add the remaining half of the butter and stir to make a sauce. Pour the sauce over the veal and serve immediately.

SERVES 4

Pesce Spada Siciliana | Sicilian-Style Grilled Swordfish

Sicilian cuisine is known for bold-tasting ingredients, such as capers, anchovies, and olives. Nuts are also a common element. Here the ingredients mingle in a ragu (sauce) to top simply grilled swordfish steaks.

⅓ cup plus ½ cup olive oil

Juice of 2 lemons

6 tablespoons chopped capers

6 tablespoons chopped fresh oregano

6 swordfish steaks, about 6 ounces each

1 cup minced onions

3 cloves garlic, minced to a paste

6 anchovy fillets

3 pints assorted colors and shapes of cherry tomatoes, stemmed

6 ounces pitted spicy olives

Salt and freshly ground black pepper to taste

3 ounces sliced almonds, toasted

MARINATE THE FISH | In a small bowl, combine ½ cup of the olive oil, the lemon juice, 3 tablespoons of the capers, and 3 tablespoons of the oregano. Place the swordfish steaks in a shallow dish and pour the marinade over the top. Turn the steaks to coat them evenly with the marinade and refrigerate for 20 minutes, or up to 3 hours.

MAKE THE TOMATO-OLIVE RAGU | In a skillet, heat the remaining ⅓ cup of the olive oil over medium heat. Add the onions, garlic, the remaining 3 tablespoons of the capers, and the anchovies and sauté until the onions are light golden brown, about 8 to 10 minutes. Add the tomatoes and sauté until the tomatoes are very soft. Add the olives and the remaining 3 tablespoons of the oregano and sauté for 2 to 3 minutes. Taste the ragu and season with salt and pepper; keep warm.

GRILL THE SWORDFISH | Preheat the grill to high (see page 41). Remove the swordfish from the marinade and grill for about 2 to 3 minutes on each side, or until the fish is cooked through.

GARNISH AND SERVE THE DISH | Transfer the swordfish to a warm platter or plates, top with the tomato-olive ragu, and garnish with the sliced almonds.

SERVES 6

Frutti di Bosco con Zabaglione | Fresh Berry Trifle with Zabaglione

This dessert can be made into individual portions or one large portion, to be served family-style, depending on the occasion. A good choice to serve at a dinner party, this dessert can be assembled ahead of time.

5 medium egg yolks

⅓ cup orange juice (about 1 orange)

¼ cup Vin Santo or similar dessert wine

3 tablespoons sugar

1¼ cups heavy cream

Sponge Cake (see page 74), cut into 1-inch cubes

18 ounces seasonal berries, such as raspberries, blackberries, blueberries, strawberries, or a combination

Whipped cream for garnish

6 strawberries, stems intact, cut into fans, for garnish

MAKE THE ZABAGLIONE BASE | Prepare a water bath by bringing about 2 inches of water to a simmer in a large pot. In a stainless steel mixing bowl, whisk together the egg yolks, orange juice, wine, and sugar and set the bowl in the pot over the simmering water. Cook, beating constantly with a hand mixer or a whisk, until the eggs triple in volume, thicken, and become a pale yellow color. When ready, the mixture should fall in ribbons from the beaters or whisk, which hold their shape on top of the sauce. Remove the bowl from the water bath and set it directly in an ice water bath. Continue to whisk until the sauce is cool.

LIGHTEN THE ZABAGLIONE BASE | In another bowl, whip the cream with a mixer or by hand until stiff peaks form. Fold the whipped cream into the base mixture until incorporated. Refrigerate the zabaglione until ready to assemble the dessert, up to 4 hours ahead of time.

MAKE INDIVIDUAL TRIFLES | Place a few cubes of cake in each of 6 footed glass dishes or soufflé dishes. Top with some of the berries and a dollop of the cold zabaglione. Continue layering the cake, berries, and zabaglione until the dishes are filled.

MAKE ONE LARGE TRIFLE | Layer the cake cubes, berries, and zabaglione in a footed trifle dish or a soufflé dish.

GARNISH AND SERVE THE TRIFLE | Pipe rosettes of whipped cream on top of the individual trifles, or around the edge of the large trifle. Garnish with the fanned strawberries.

SERVES 6

Cannoli Moderna
Contemporary Cannoli

Cannoli shells are traditionally shaped into cylinders into which a rich ricotta and cream mixture is piped. In this contemporary version of cannoli, the shells are shaped into disks and layered with the ricotta mixture as if making a Napoleon.

1½ cups all-purpose flour

2 teaspoons sugar, plus more to taste

1 teaspoon unsweetened cocoa powder, plus more for dusting, if desired

2 tablespoons olive oil

¼ cup Marsala wine

1 pound ricotta cheese

8 ounces whole almonds, toasted

8 ounces semisweet chocolate, chopped

6 tablespoons amaretto

Confectioners' sugar (optional)

Homemade or purchased chocolate sauce (optional)

MAKE THE CANNOLI DOUGH | Sift the flour, sugar, and cocoa powder. In a food processor or working by hand, add the oil and wine to the sifted dry ingredients and mix until the dough comes together in a ball. Wrap the dough with plastic wrap and let it stand at room temperature for 30 minutes.

ROLL OUT THE CANNOLI DOUGH | Preheat the oven to 450°F. With a rolling pin or pasta machine, roll out the dough into thin sheets about ⅛-inch thick. With a 2½- to 3-inch cutter, cut the dough into eighteen circles. Transfer the circles to a well-greased baking sheet.

BAKE THE CANNOLI SHELLS | Top the dough circles with a second baking sheet. Place the baking sheets in the oven and bake the circles until golden brown and blistered, about 15 to 18 minutes. Transfer the circles to a rack to cool.

MAKE THE FILLING | In a food processor or by hand, mix the ricotta, almonds, chocolate, and amaretto until evenly blended. Taste the filling and sweeten to taste with sugar.

ASSEMBLE THE CANNOLI AND SERVE | Place the filling mixture in a pastry bag without a tip. For each portion, place 1 cannoli circle on a dessert plate. Pipe some of the filling mixture on top of the circle and top with another cannoli circle. Pipe on another layer of filling and top with a third cannoli circle. Dust the top layer with confectioners' sugar and/or cocoa powder. Serve with chocolate sauce if desired.

SERVES 6

Mediterranean

The Mediterranean diet has been praised for its healthfulness and bright, bold flavors. Small dishes are important in this cuisine, which can be eaten in moderate portions several times over the course of a day, or combined for a heartier meal. They're often perfumed with mysterious spices, but rich sauces and too much fat never overwhelm them.

On the following pages you'll find a selection of recipes from all over the Mediterranean region, from the sunny seashores of Greece, to the dunes of North Africa, to the warm beaches of coastal Spain.

Cod and Potato Fritters with Aioli

Salt cod and potatoes are the main ingredients in Spanish *bacalo*. Here they appear in a different guise—as hot crispy fritters—to be dipped into the thick garlicky mayonnaise *aioli* and eaten hot.

1½ cups olive oil

1 onion, cut into small dice

2 pounds salt cod

6 pounds russet potatoes

4 to 4½ cups dried bread crumbs

1 cup heavy cream

4 eggs, beaten until frothy

Grated zest and juice of 5 lemons, or more to taste

Leaves from 1 bunch fresh dill, minced, or more to taste

Freshly ground black pepper to taste

¾ cup self-rising flour

Egg wash: 3 eggs beaten with 2 tablespoons water

Aioli (recipe follows)

SAUTÉ THE ONION | In a small skillet, heat ¼ cup of the olive oil over medium heat. Add the onion and sauté until translucent; cool to room temperature.

COOK THE SALT COD AND POTATOES | Bring a large pot of water to a boil. Rinse the salt cod in cold water to remove the excess salt. Drop the salt cod into the boiling water and boil for 15 to 20 minutes, until it is soft. While the cod is cooking, simmer the potatoes in salted water until tender.

MIX THE FRITTER MIXTURE | Drain the salt cod and cool it until just cool enough to handle, but still quite warm. With your fingertips, shred the cod into fine pieces, removing any bones or cartilage, and place them in a bowl. Drain the potatoes and add them to the bowl with the salt cod. Working by hand, blend the potatoes until they are broken up. Add 2 to 2½ cups of the bread crumbs, the cream, eggs, sautéed onion, lemon zest, lemon juice, dill, and pepper and continue to mix until evenly blended. Place the flour, egg wash, and the remaining bread crumbs in separate shallow bowls.

MAKE A TEST PORTION | Shape the salt cod mixture into a small cake. Dredge the cake in the flour, shaking off the excess. Then, dredge the cake in the egg wash, letting the excess drip back into the bowl. Finally, coat the cake with the bread crumbs. In a skillet, heat the remaining olive oil over medium-high heat until it reaches 375°F. Add the cake and fry for about 2 minutes on the first side, until well browned, adjusting the heat if necessary. Turn the cake and cook on the other side for 2 to 3 minutes. Drain the cake briefly on paper towels. Taste the cake and check it for consistency. If the consistency seems too loose, add more bread crumbs to the fritter mixture. Adjust the seasoning as necessary with pepper, lemon juice, or dill.

SHAPE AND PAN-FRY THE FRITTERS | Shape and cook the remaining cod mixture in the same manner as the test portion. Keep the fritters warm in a 250°F oven until ready to serve. Serve with the Aioli for dipping.

MAKES 16 TO 18 FRITTERS

Aioli

2 egg yolks (see Chef's Tip)

4 cloves garlic, minced to a paste

1½ teaspoons white wine vinegar

1½ teaspoons water

1 teaspoon dry mustard

2 cups extra-virgin olive oil

Salt and freshly ground black pepper to taste

Lemon juice to taste

In a food processor or working by hand, combine the egg yolks, garlic, vinegar, water, and mustard and process or whisk until slightly foamy. While processing or whisking, add the olive oil in a thin stream until the mixture is blended and thickened. Taste the aioli and season with salt, pepper, and lemon juice.

➤ CHEF'S TIP

If you are concerned about the raw eggs in your area, substitute an equal amount of pasteurized egg yolks, available in the frozen food or dairy section of your supermarket.

Tunisian Melaoui | Unleavened Semolina Griddle Bread

This traditional North African griddle bread uses a unique cooking process. The loaves are cooked in a stack, utilizing steam heat to cook one side of the bread, and the heat from the pan to cook the other side. The semolina lends a nutty flavor to the loaves.

1 pound semolina (see Chef's Tip)

1 teaspoon salt

1¼ cups cold water

¼ cup olive oil, plus more as needed

¼ cup ground cumin

MAKE THE DOUGH | Combine the semolina, salt, water, and oil. In a food processor, with a mixer, or by hand, beat the dough until smooth and elastic. Form the dough into a round in the bowl.

SHAPE THE DOUGH | Coat the bowl and the dough with a small amount of olive oil to prevent it from sticking. You may also need to coat your hands with oil while working with the dough. Divide the dough into 6 equal pieces and form the pieces into 6 balls. Using your hands or a tortilla press, flatten one ball of dough until about ⅛-inch thick and 8 to 10 inches in diameter.

COOK THE FIRST LAYER OF BREAD | Preheat a nonstick grill pan or skillet over medium heat for 5 minutes. Place a flattened piece of dough in the pan and sprinkle the top with ground cumin. Cook for about 3 minutes, or until the underside has well-formed grill marks.

BEGIN TO LAYER THE BREAD | While the first dough portion is cooking, flatten a second round of dough. Flip the first portion of dough and immediately cover with the second round of dough. Sprinkle the top with cumin and cook for 3 minutes. The steam from the first piece of dough will cook the underside of the second piece of dough. While the dough is cooking, flatten a third piece of dough. Flip over the second dough layer to cook directly on the grill pan; lay the third piece of dough over the top. Continue flattening, layering, and cooking the dough until you have a stack of 6 loaves. As you add layers, each bread will take a little longer to cook, up to 5 minutes. Serve immediately.

MAKES 6 LOAVES

► CHEF'S TIP
Look for semolina in a health food store or specialty market. It may be located in the bulk section.

Carrot Salad with Radishes and Oranges

Sweet oranges and peppery radishes are good foils to a carrot salad flavored with cinnamon and cayenne pepper. Orange flower water adds a mysterious flavor, and Italian parsley lends a fresh accent.

1½ tablespoons lemon juice

3 tablespoons extra-virgin olive oil

Pinch of ground cinnamon

2 teaspoons sugar

1 teaspoon orange flower water (see Chef's Tips)

Salt and cayenne pepper to taste

3 oranges

8 carrots, cut into large julienne

9 radishes, sliced

1 tablespoon coarsely chopped fresh Italian parsley

MAKE THE DRESSING | In a bowl, whisk together the lemon juice, oil, cinnamon, sugar, and orange flower water. Season the dressing with salt and cayenne; set aside.

CUT THE ORANGES | Cut the stem and blossom end from the oranges so that they sit flat on the cutting board. Using a sharp knife, slice away the peel and white pith from each orange, exposing the flesh below. Working over a bowl, cut between the membranes to free each orange segment, dropping the segments into the bowl as you work.

TOSS AND SERVE THE SALAD | Add the carrots and radishes to the bowl and toss the ingredients until well mixed. Taste and adjust the seasonings. Serve the salad immediately garnished with the parsley.

SERVES 6

➤ CHEF'S TIPS

Orange flower water is distilled from the blossoms of bitter orange trees. Look for it in small brown bottles in a specialty food store.

To save prep time, you can use the julienne disk of a food processor to cut the carrots.

Beet and Orange Salad with Anise and Walnuts

Anise seeds offer an intriguing hint of licorice to this salad of earthy roasted beets, tangy fresh oranges, and crunchy toasted walnuts. Roasting beets intensifies their natural sweetness and retains their nutrients.

1 pound beets, washed well

½ teaspoon anise seeds

3 whole cloves

½ teaspoon salt

⅛ teaspoon freshly ground black pepper

2 tablespoons sherry vinegar

¼ cup extra-virgin olive oil

¼ cup orange juice

2 tablespoons red wine vinegar

Salt and freshly ground black pepper to taste

2 cups mixed lettuces, such as frisee and romaine

3 oranges, peeled and cut into ¼-inch-thick slices

½ cup walnuts, toasted and coarsely chopped

2 tablespoons coarsely chopped fresh Italian parsley

ROAST THE BEETS | Preheat the oven to 350°F. Place the beets on a large sheet of aluminum foil and sprinkle with the anise, cloves, salt, pepper, sherry vinegar, and 2 tablespoons of the oil. Wrap the foil around the beets. Place the beets in the oven and roast for about 45 minutes, depending on the size of the beets, until they are easily pierced with a knife. With a paring knife, remove the peels from the beets and cut them into bite-sized wedges; set aside.

MAKE THE DRESSING | In a bowl, whisk together the orange juice, red wine vinegar, and the remaining 2 tablespoons of the oil. Season the dressing with salt and pepper; set aside.

ASSEMBLE AND SERVE THE SALAD | Arrange the greens on a serving platter or plates. Arrange the orange slices decoratively on top of the greens and top with the beets and walnuts. Drizzle the salad with the dressing and sprinkle with salt, pepper, and chopped parsley. Serve immediately.

SERVES 6

➤ CHEF'S TIP
Wear plastic gloves when handling beets if you don't want their pink juices to stain your hands.

Orange Salad with Olives and Cilantro

Two types of oranges combine with olives and preserved lemons for a nice sampling of North African flavors and an explosion of bright colors. Choose good-quality olives; an inferior variety will make an inferior salad.

¼ cup orange juice

2 tablespoons red wine vinegar

3 tablespoons extra-virgin olive oil

Salt and cayenne pepper to taste

⅓ cup shaved red onion

3 oranges, peeled and cut into ¼-inch-thick slices

3 blood oranges, peeled and cut into ¼-inch-thick slices

⅓ cup sliced black olives

2 tablespoons preserved lemon peel, finely diced (see Chef's Tip)

3 tablespoons chopped fresh cilantro

MAKE THE DRESSING | In a bowl, whisk together the orange juice, 1 tablespoon of the vinegar, and the oil. Season the dressing with salt and cayenne; set aside.

SOAK THE ONION | Place the onion in a bowl with the remaining 1 tablespoon vinegar and let stand until the color turns vivid red, about 10 minutes.

ASSEMBLE AND SERVE THE SALAD | Arrange the oranges, overlapping and alternating colors, on a serving platter or plates. Top with the olives and preserved lemon peel. Drizzle the dressing over the top and sprinkle with cilantro. Serve immediately.

SERVES 6

➤ CHEF'S TIP

Preserved lemons, lemons pickled in salt, lemon juice, and spices, are a common ingredient in Moroccan cuisine. Look for them in a Moroccan market or specialty food store.

Chorizo-Filled Dates Wrapped with Bacon

For a special indulgence, you can coat these Spanish *tapas* in flour, then in egg wash and fry them in 380°F oil until golden brown. Drain them briefly on paper towels and serve hot.

2 Spanish chorizo sausages
(about 4 ounces)

24 pitted dates

6 slices bacon, cut into quarters

FILL THE DATES WITH CHORIZO | Remove the casings from the chorizo sausages and cut them into 24 small sticks the length of the dates. Press one piece of chorizo into each date and mold the date around the chorizo.

WRAP THE DATES WITH BACON | Wrap each date with a piece of bacon and set it seam-side down on a baking sheet.

BAKE THE AND SERVE THE TAPAS | When ready to serve, preheat the oven to 375°F. Bake the bacon-wrapped dates until the bacon is crisp, about 8 to 12 minutes. Drain the dates briefly on paper towels and serve while still very hot.

SERVES 12 AS AN APPETIZER

Stewed Lamb and Chickpeas

Pancetta, chorizo, garlic, and North African spices enliven this thick stew of tender lamb leg meat and chickpeas. Orange and lemon zests provide a tangy counterpoint to the stew.

2 tablespoons olive oil

4 ounces pancetta, cut into small dice (see Chef's Tip, page 85)

1 large onion, cut into small dice

4 cloves garlic, minced

12 ounces dried chickpeas (garbanzo beans), soaked overnight in water to cover by 3 inches

14 ounces lamb leg meat, cut into 1-inch cubes

Water or stock

½ teaspoon ground coriander

½ teaspoon cumin

Pinch of turmeric

2 carrots, diced

1 leek, white and light green parts, sliced

Grated zests of 1 orange and 1 lemon

Salt and freshly ground white pepper to taste

5 ounces chorizo, sliced

SAUTÉ THE PANCETTA, ONION, AND GARLIC | In a heavy-bottomed saucepan or stockpot, heat the oil over medium-high heat. Add the pancetta, onion, and garlic and sauté until the onion is translucent.

SIMMER THE LAMB WITH THE BEANS | Drain the chickpeas, rinse them thoroughly, and place in a large pot. Add the lamb and water or stock to just cover the meat; stir briefly. Bring the mixture to a boil over high heat. Reduce the heat to low and simmer gently for 40 minutes, stirring occasionally. Stir in the coriander, cumin, and turmeric and simmer for 20 minutes, adding more water or stock as needed to cover the mixture.

ADD THE REMAINING INGREDIENTS | Add the carrots, leek, and citrus zests. Taste the stew, season with salt and pepper, and simmer for 20 minutes. Stir in the chorizo and simmer until the chorizo is heated through. Taste the stew again and adjust the seasonings. Serve hot.

SERVES 6 TO 8

Sautéed Chicken with Moroccan Hot and Sweet Tomato Sauce

The intriguing tomato sauce, redolent of honey and spices, is a wonderful change of pace for serving over boneless chicken breasts. Use homemade or purchased tomato sauce and enhance it with North African flavors.

1 onion, chopped

2 cloves garlic, finely minced

2 tablespoons butter

¾ teaspoon ground cinnamon

¼ teaspoon ground ginger

¼ teaspoon cayenne pepper, or to taste

2 cups tomato sauce

2 tablespoons dark honey

Salt and freshly ground black pepper to taste

8 boneless, skinless chicken breast halves

3 tablespoons olive oil

2 tablespoons sesame seeds, toasted

2 tablespoons chopped fresh cilantro leaves

MAKE THE TOMATO SAUCE | In a food processor, process the onion and garlic until a coarse paste forms. In a saucepan, heat the butter over medium heat. Add the onion-garlic puree and sauté for about 10 minutes, or until tender. Stir in the cinnamon, ginger, and cayenne and sauté for 2 to 3 minutes. Add the tomato sauce and honey and simmer for 5 minutes. Taste and season with salt and pepper.

BROWN THE CHICKEN | Preheat the oven to 350°F. Blot the chicken dry with paper towels and season with salt and pepper. In a skillet, heat half of the olive oil over medium-high heat. Add half of the chicken pieces to the pan and sauté on one side for about 2 to 3 minutes, until browned. Turn the chicken over and sauté on the second side for another 3 minutes, until browned. Reduce the heat if necessary to avoid scorching the chicken. Transfer the chicken to a baking dish. Repeat the browning process with the remaining oil and chicken and transfer it to the baking dish.

BAKE THE CHICKEN WITH THE SAUCE | Spoon the sauce over the chicken and bake it for 15 minutes, or until the chicken is cooked through (the internal temperature should be at least 180°F).

GARNISH AND SERVE THE DISH | Sprinkle the chicken with the sesame seeds and cilantro and divide it among serving plates. Serve hot.

SERVES 8

Albóndigas en Salsa de Almendra | Meatballs in Almond Sauce

The people of Spain eat many small dishes or *tapas*, around which a whole cooking repertoire has been developed. Boldly flavored, here is an example of a common *tapa* you might find in that country.

15 cloves garlic

1 cup fresh white bread crumbs

1½ cups dry white wine

¾ pound ground beef

1 pound ground pork

1 pound ground veal

2 eggs

7 tablespoons minced fresh Italian parsley

Salt and freshly ground black pepper to taste

3 tablespoons olive oil

1 onion, minced

1 carrot, minced

30 whole blanched almonds

2 cups beef broth (homemade or low-sodium canned)

¾ cup fresh or frozen peas

3 green onions, minced

1 bay leaf

PREPARE THE GARLIC | Mince 5 of the garlic cloves to a fine paste and set aside. Slice the remaining 10 cloves very thinly and set aside separately.

MAKE THE MEATBALL MIXTURE | In a large mixing bowl, combine the bread crumbs with ¼ cup of the wine and let them soak for 15 minutes. Add the meats, eggs, minced garlic, one-half of the parsley, the salt and pepper. Mix the mixture with a wooden spoon until evenly blended. Shape the mixture into small meatballs.

BROWN THE MEATBALLS | In a large skillet or flameproof casserole, heat the oil over medium-high heat. In batches if necessary to avoid overcrowding, add the meatballs to the pan and cook until evenly browned on all sides, about 12 to 15 minutes. Transfer the meatballs to a platter.

MAKE THE SAUCE | Add the onion and carrot to the skillet and sauté over medium-high heat until the onion is translucent, about 10 minutes. Add the remaining 1¼ cups of the wine and stir to scrape up the browned bits from the bottom of the pan. Add the sliced garlic and continue to cook until the liquid has nearly all reduced. In a food processor, process the almonds to a fine paste. With the machine running, add the beef broth in a gradual stream until blended. Pour the almond mixture into the pan with the onions and carrots. Bring the mixture to a simmer.

FINISH COOKING THE MEATBALLS AND SERVE | Return the meatballs to the pan. Add the peas, the remaining half of the parsley, the green onions, and bay leaf. Bring the sauce back to a bare simmer over low heat and cook for about 45 minutes, until the meatballs are cooked through. Taste the sauce and season with salt and pepper. Divide the meatballs and sauce among serving plates. Serve hot.

SERVES 10 TO 12 AS AN APPETIZER

Fideo with Chicken and Sausage

Made in the same fashion as risotto, these hearty noodles are infused with broth a little at a time until the correct texture is achieved. If you can't find fideo, substitute vermicelli (thin pasta strands).

¼ cup olive oil

6 ounces bulk Italian sausage

2 onions, chopped

1 red bell pepper, seeded and cut into thin strips

1 green Anaheim chile, seeded and cut into thin strips

3 bay leaves

3 tomatoes, peeled, seeded and diced (see Chef's Tip, page 8)

3 cloves garlic, minced

18 hazelnuts, toasted and skinned

1 tablespoon minced fresh Italian parsley, plus more for garnish

½ slice bread, fried

¾ teaspoons Spanish paprika

¼ teaspoon saffron, soaked in 1 tablespoon water

14 ounces Fideo noodles

5 cups chicken broth

Salt and freshly ground black pepper to taste

5 boneless chicken breast halves

⅓ cup freshly grated Parmesan cheese

MAKE THE SAUCE BASE | In a shallow 12-inch skillet or flameproof casserole, heat 2 tablespoons of the oil over medium-high heat. Add the sausage and sauté for about 5 minutes, until lightly browned and crumbly. Add the onions, pepper, chile, and bay leaves and sauté for 5 minutes. Add the tomatoes and simmer until most of the liquid has evaporated, about 5 to 10 minutes.

THICKEN THE SAUCE BASE | In a food processor, or with a mortar and pestle, mix the garlic, hazelnuts, parsley, bread, paprika, and saffron until the garlic and nuts are both ground to a uniform paste. Add the nut mixture (picada) to the pan and sauté until its aroma is apparent.

COOK THE NOODLES IN THE SAUCE | Add the noodles to the skillet and stir to coat well with the sauce. In a saucepan, bring the chicken broth to a simmer. Add about half of the hot broth to the fideo mixture and stir well. Reduce the heat if necessary so that the mixture stays at a simmer. Cook, stirring occasionally, until the liquid is absorbed. Continue cooking in this manner, adding broth 1 cup at a time, until the liquid is absorbed and the noodles are tender. (You may not need to add all of the broth, depending on the size and brand of the noodles and how fast you cook them.) Taste the mixture and season with salt and pepper. When the noodles are tender and still slightly liquid (they will continue to absorb broth), remove the dish from the heat and let it stand for 5 minutes.

SAUTÉ THE CHICKEN | Season the chicken breasts with salt and pepper. In a skillet, heat the remaining 2 tablespoons olive oil over medium heat. Add the chicken breasts and sauté until they are cooked through (180°F), crisp, and golden brown.

GARNISH AND SERVE THE DISH | Place the cooked chicken on top of the noodles, sprinkle with the cheese, and garnish with parsley.

SERVES 10

Moussaka

Though lamb is traditional in this Greek specialty, you can substitute beef, turkey, pork, or a combination of meats in the meat sauce. For an elegant presentation, assemble the layers in a springform pan. Invert the moussaka onto a serving platter and cut it into wedges.

3 eggplants

Salt

⅓ cup olive oil, or as needed

3 onions, diced

1¼ pounds ground lamb

2 cups chopped canned plum tomatoes with juice

3 cloves garlic

4 whole cloves

Small piece cinnamon stick, or ¼ teaspoon ground cinnamon

1 bay leaf

Pinch ground allspice

Salt and freshly ground black pepper to taste

½ cup water

2 tablespoons tomato paste

¼ cup dry red wine (optional)

5 tablespoons butter

5 tablespoons all-purpose flour

2½ cups milk

Freshly grated nutmeg to taste

2 egg yolks

¼ cup plain bread crumbs (optional)

½ cup grated kefalotyri or Parmesan cheese

PREPARE THE EGGPLANT | Cut off the stems and tips from the eggplants and cut them into slices about ½-inch thick. Place the eggplant slices in a colander and sprinkle liberally with salt. Place the colander in a large bowl or in the sink to drain for about 45 minutes. Rinse the eggplant well and blot it dry with paper towels.

SAUTÉ THE EGGPLANT | In a large nonstick or cast iron skillet, heat about 1 tablespoon of the olive oil. In batches, add the eggplant slices and sauté for about 2 to 3 minutes on each side, adding more oil as necessary. Drain the sautéed eggplant on paper towels.

MAKE THE MEAT SAUCE | In a large skillet, heat 1 tablespoon of the olive oil over medium-high heat. Add the onions and sauté until translucent, about 15 to 20 minutes. Add the ground lamb and sauté until it is crumbly and no pink remains. Add the tomatoes, garlic, cloves, cinnamon, bay leaf, allspice, salt, pepper, and water. Bring the mixture to a simmer and simmer for 45 minutes. Stir in the tomato paste and red wine, if desired, and simmer for another 10 minutes, until the sauce is very thick and well flavored.

MAKE THE BÉCHAMEL SAUCE | In a saucepan, heat the butter over medium heat. Add the flour and cook, stirring, for about 5 minutes. Gradually whisk in the milk, taking care to work out any lumps that form. Bring the milk to a full boil over high heat. Reduce the heat to low and simmer gently, stirring frequently, for 30 minutes, or until the sauce is thickened. Remove the sauce from the heat, stir in the nutmeg, and season with salt and pepper. In a small bowl, whisk the egg yolks. Add a small amount of the hot sauce to the bowl with the yolks and blend well. Transfer the contents of the bowl to the pan, stir well and keep warm.

ASSEMBLE THE MOUSSAKA | Preheat the oven to 350°F. Scatter the bread crumbs, if using, in a deep, rectangular baking dish. Layer half of the eggplant slices over the bread crumbs. Pour in the meat sauce and spread it evenly. Layer the remaining eggplant over the meat sauce. Pour the béchamel over the eggplant and spread it evenly. Sprinkle with the cheese.

BAKE AND SERVE THE MOUSSAKA | Place the moussaka in the oven and bake for about 1 hour, or until the béchamel is thick and golden brown. Let the moussaka stand at room temperature for about 20 minutes before cutting into serving portions.

SERVES 12 TO 14

Shrimp with Tomatoes, Oregano, and Feta Cheese

Briny shrimp are spiked with the sunny Greek flavors of oregano, tomatoes and feta cheese. Take care not to overcook the shrimp when sautéing or they will become rubbery after being flashed under the broiler.

1½ pounds large shrimp, peeled and deveined

1 teaspoon salt, plus more to taste

¼ teaspoon freshly ground black pepper, plus more to taste

¼ cup olive oil

1 onion, chopped

4 cloves garlic, minced

¼ teaspoon cayenne pepper

2 tablespoons chopped fresh oregano

1 cup Fresh Tomato Sauce (see page 15)

Red chile flakes or cayenne pepper to taste

1 teaspoon sugar

½ pound feta cheese

¼ cup chopped fresh Italian parsley

Sliced crusty bread

SAUTÉ THE SHRIMP | Sprinkle the shrimp with the salt and pepper. In a large skillet, heat 2 tablespoons of the oil over medium heat. Add the shrimp to the pan and sauté until they just turn pink, about 3 minutes. Remove the shrimp with a slotted spoon and distribute them equally among four ovenproof ramekins.

MAKE THE SAUCE | Add the remaining 2 tablespoons oil to the skillet. Add the onion and sauté over medium heat until tender. Add the garlic, cayenne, and oregano and sauté for 2 minutes. Add the Fresh Tomato Sauce and simmer for a few minutes. Taste the sauce and season with the chile flakes or cayenne, sugar, salt and pepper. Pour the sauce over the shrimp in the ramekins.

SPRINKLE WITH CHEESE, BROIL, AND SERVE | When ready to serve, preheat the broiler. Crumble the feta cheese over the sauce in the ramekins. Place the ramekins under the broiler and broil until the cheese melts. Sprinkle with parsley and serve accompanied by crusty bread.

SERVES 4

Chocolate Baklava

> For a fresh take on the classic Greek sweet, chocolate and almonds are added to the traditional baklava fillings of walnuts, honey, and spices. Plan ahead, as the dessert takes awhile to assemble and bake.

2 cups slivered almonds, toasted and coarsely chopped

2 cups walnuts, toasted and coarsely chopped

1½ cups miniature chocolate chips

1½ tablespoons ground cinnamon

½ teaspoon ground cloves

2½ tablespoons unsweetened cocoa powder

3 tablespoons butter, melted

Pinch of salt

2 cups water

2 cups sugar

3 strips lemon zest

One 4-inch cinnamon stick

½ teaspoon lemon juice, or to taste

¾ cup honey

1 cup butter, melted

One 1 pound package phyllo pastry (see Chef's Tip, page 151)

¼ cup whole cloves

⅓ cup water

MAKE THE FILLING | In a food processor or by hand, mix together the almonds, walnuts, chocolate chips, cinnamon, cloves, cocoa powder, 3 tablespoons melted butter, and the salt; set aside at room temperature until needed.

MAKE THE SYRUP | In a 2-quart saucepan, mix the water, sugar, zest, and cinnamon stick and bring to a boil over high heat. Boil for about 8 minutes or until the mixture thickens to a syrup consistency. Remove the zest and the cinnamon from the syrup and stir in the lemon juice and honey; set the syrup aside at room temperature until needed.

ASSEMBLE THE BAKLAVA | Preheat the oven to 350°F. Brush a 9-x-13-inch baking pan with melted butter and lay one sheet of phyllo pastry into the bottom and up the sides of the pan. Brush the phyllo with melted butter and lay a second sheet of phyllo on top. Continue the brushing and layering process until there are 12 layers of buttered pastry. Spread half of the filling over the pastry layers. Smooth the filling evenly, then press it down firmly. Top the filling with 5 more sheets of pastry, brushing each with butter as it is layered. Spread the remaining half of the filling over the pastry, smooth it evenly, and press it down firmly. Top the filling with 12 more sheets of pastry, brushing each with butter as it is layered. Cut away any pastry that extends up the sides of the baking pan so that the top of the dessert is flat.

SCORE THE BAKLAVA | Using a knife and a ruler, cut the baklava into 8 lengthwise strips, cutting all the way through to the bottom of the pan. In the same manner, make a series of parallel cuts diagonally across the first to create diamond shapes. Place a single clove in the middle of each diamond shape and sprinkle the water over the top.

BAKE AND SERVE THE BAKLAVA | Place the baklava in the oven and bake for about 1 hour, or until the pastry is crisp and a rich golden color. Remove the baklava from the oven and pour the syrup evenly over the entire surface of the baklava. Let it stand for at least 30 minutes before eating. Serve at room temperature.

SERVES 15 TO 20

Healthy

cooking is no longer an alternative concept, rather, it is increasingly becoming a way of life in this country. Often we are looking to other cultures' cuisines, such as Japan, China, Thailand, India, and Italy, where the dishes are low in fat, but full of flavor, to influence our daily meal choices.

This chapter offers a range of internationally inspired healthy dishes—a few of them homegrown—along with useful tips on keeping these and other dishes healthy in your daily lives. You'll find these recipes suitable for everyday meals, and even special occasion feasts.

Spicy Asian Grilled Shrimp and Marinated Vegetable Salad

Asian cuisines are known for bold flavors and very little fat. Here marinated shrimp is quickly grilled and served over a nutritious vegetable salad that is spiked with a lively soy vinaigrette.

24 medium shrimp, peeled

3 tablespoons plus 2 teaspoons rice vinegar

3 teaspoons minced garlic

¾ teaspoon Chinese five-spice powder

¾ teaspoon minced fresh ginger

½ teaspoon Thai fish sauce (nam pla)

½ teaspoon Tabasco sauce

½ teaspoon toasted sesame oil

⅓ cup vegetable broth

2 teaspoons low-sodium soy sauce

2 teaspoons minced shallots

2 teaspoons grainy mustard

⅓ cup peanut oil

1 tablespoon chopped fresh chives

1½ cups julienned carrot

1½ cups julienned daikon radish

2 tablespoons minced pickled ginger

Julienned toasted nori (seaweed) for garnish (optional)

Toasted black and white sesame seeds for garnish (optional)

BUTTERFLY AND MARINATE THE SHRIMP | With a sharp paring knife, make a horizontal cut lengthwise down the back of each shrimp, cutting almost but not entirely through the shrimp. Remove and discard the dark vein that runs down the length of the shrimp. Place the shrimp in a glass bowl. Add 2 teaspoons of the vinegar, 1½ teaspoons of the garlic, the five-spice powder, ginger, Tabasco, fish sauce, and oil to the bowl. Cover the bowl and refrigerate for at least 1 hour.

MARINATE THE VEGETABLES | In a medium bowl, combine the broth, the remaining 3 tablespoons vinegar, the soy sauce, shallots, mustard, and remaining 1½ tablespoons garlic. While whisking, slowly drizzle in the oil until blended. Stir in the chives. Add the carrot, daikon, and pickled ginger to the bowl and toss well. Cover the bowl and refrigerate for at least 30 minutes.

GRILL THE SHRIMP | Preheat a gas or charcoal grill to medium (see page 41). Drain the shrimp and place them on the grill. Grill the shrimp until thoroughly cooked, about 2 minutes per side; take care not to overcook.

SERVE THE DISH | Drain the marinated vegetables and divide them among 4 or 6 serving plates. Arrange the grilled shrimp on top the vegetables and serve immediately garnished with the nori and sesame seeds, if desired.

SERVES 6 AS AN APPETIZER, OR 4 AS A MAIN COURSE

➤ CHEF'S TIPS

Look for the fish sauce, pickled ginger, nori, and black sesame seeds in an Asian market, specialty food store, or the international aisle of a good-quality supermarket.

To save prep time, you can use the julienne disk of a food processor to cut the vegetables.

Chorizo and Vegetable Soup

There's just enough chorizo, spicy Mexican sausage, in this soup to add flavor without adding much extra fat. Though top-quality ingredients are essential, this is a good recipe to make when you have a bounty of vegetables on hand.

2 ½ ounces chorizo, casings removed, diced

1½ teaspoons olive oil

¼ cup diced onion

2 tablespoons diced celery

1 teaspoon minced garlic

¾ teaspoon cumin seeds

2½ cups chicken broth

2 cups peeled, seeded, and diced tomatoes (see Chef's Tip, page 8)

1 medium white or yellow potato, peeled and diced

1 small red bell pepper, diced

1 small green pepper, diced

1 tablespoon tomato paste

½ bay leaf

1 tablespoon chopped fresh Italian parsley

¼ teaspoon chopped dried oregano

¼ teaspoon salt

1 cup corn kernels

¼ teaspoon freshly ground black pepper

1 tablespoon chopped fresh cilantro

SAUTÉ THE CHORIZO | Heat a large saucepan over medium-high heat. Add the chorizo and sauté until browned, about 5 to 10 minutes. Transfer the chorizo to paper towels to drain, and discard the fat from the pan.

SAUTÉ THE AROMATICS | Add the oil to the pan over medium heat. Add the onion, celery, garlic, and cumin seeds and sauté until the onion is translucent, about 5 minutes.

SIMMER THE SOUP | Add the chorizo, broth, tomatoes, potato, peppers, tomato paste, bay leaf, half of the parsley, the oregano, and salt and bring to a boil over high heat. Reduce the heat to low and simmer until the potatoes are tender, about 20 minutes. Discard the bay leaf. Stir in the corn and black pepper and simmer until heated through.

GARNISH AND SERVE THE SOUP | Ladle the soup into warm soup bowls and garnish with the cilantro and remaining parsley.

SERVES 4 TO 6

Portobello Mushrooms with Tuscan Bean Salad and Celery Juice

Here is a satisfying entrée salad that won't spoil a healthy eating regimen. The colorful bean-vegetable salad enhanced with meaty portobello mushrooms is also suited for vegetarian diners.

⅓ cup dried cannellini beans, soaked overnight in water to cover by 3 inches

2 to 3 cups vegetable broth or water

¼ cup finely diced carrot

¼ cup finely diced celery

¼ cup finely diced red bell pepper

¼ cup finely diced yellow bell pepper

2 tablespoons thinly sliced green onion tops

½ cup Champagne Vinaigrette (recipe follows)

1 tablespoon chopped fresh chives

1 tablespoon chopped fresh Italian parsley

½ teaspoon salt

¼ teaspoon freshly ground black pepper

4 medium portobello mushroom caps, wiped clean

1 tablespoon olive oil

⅓ cup shredded radicchio

2 teaspoons chopped fresh cilantro

½ cup celery juice (see Chef's Tip)

COOK THE BEANS | Drain the beans and rinse them with cold water. Combine the beans and 2 cups of the broth in a large saucepan and bring to a simmer. Simmer until the beans are tender, 40 minutes to 1 hour. Add more liquid as necessary to keep the beans submerged during cooking. Turn off the heat and let the beans cool in the cooking liquid.

MARINATE THE BEANS AND VEGETABLES | Drain the beans and transfer them to a bowl. Add the carrot, celery, red pepper, yellow pepper, green onion tops, Champagne Vinaigrette, chives, parsley, salt, and pepper and toss well to mix the ingredients. Let the mixture stand at room temperature for 2 hours to blend the flavors.

ROAST THE MUSHROOMS | Preheat the oven to 350°F. Place the mushroom caps on a baking sheet and brush them with the olive oil. Cover the pan with foil and roast the mushrooms until tender, about 15 to 20 minutes. Increase the oven temperature to broil. Remove the foil from the pan and broil the mushrooms for about 2 minutes on each side, until browned.

GARNISH AND SERVE THE DISH | Divide the bean salad among 4 small plates, mounding the salad in the center of the plate. Cut each mushroom cap into ½-inch-thick slices and arrange the slices around the bean salad. Garnish each plate with radicchio and cilantro, and drizzle with the celery juice. Serve immediately.

SERVES 4 AS AN APPETIZER

► CHEF'S TIP

Celery juice can be prepared at home if you have a juicer, or it look for it in a health food store or juice bar.

Champagne Vinaigrette

¾ *teaspoon cornstarch*

½ *cup vegetable broth*

¼ *cup Champagne vinegar*

¼ *cup extra-virgin olive oil*

2 *tablespoons finely chopped fresh basil*

Pinch of salt

In a small bowl or cup, mix the cornstarch with 2 teaspoons of the broth and stir until smooth. In a saucepan, bring the remaining broth to a boil and stir in the cornstarch mixture. Cook, stirring constantly, until the broth has thickened. Remove the mixture from the heat, stir in the vinegar, and cool completely. While whisking, slowly drizzle in the oil until incorporated. Stir in the basil and salt and refrigerate until needed. Whisk the dressing just before serving.

Artichoke Salad

When maintaining a healthy eating regimen, choose highly flavored foods, such as olives and sharp cheeses, so that even when used sparingly, their inclusion in a dish adds great dimension.

1 teaspoon anchovy paste

½ teaspoon cornstarch

⅓ cup vegetable broth

3 tablespoons red wine vinegar

3 tablespoons extra-virgin olive oil

¼ teaspoon dried oregano

¼ teaspoon freshly ground black pepper

1 cup frozen artichoke hearts, thawed and quartered

½ cup green peas, cooked if fresh, thawed if frozen

⅓ cup julienned carrot

¼ cup picholine olives, pitted and cut into slivers

¼ cup niçoise olives, pitted and cut into slivers

3 cups mesclun greens (about 6 ounces)

2 tablespoons freshly grated Asiago cheese

1 tablespoon chopped fresh Italian parsley

MAKE THE DRESSING | In a small bowl, blend the anchovy paste, cornstarch, and 1 tablespoon of the broth. Bring the remaining broth to a boil in a small saucepan and add the anchovy mixture, stirring constantly until thickened. Remove from the heat, stir in the vinegar, and cool completely. When the mixture is cool, gradually whisk in the oil until blended. Stir in the oregano and pepper.

MARINATE THE VEGETABLES | In a bowl, combine the artichokes, peas, carrot, and olives. Stir in the dressing and toss to coat the vegetables well. Cover the bowl and let the vegetables marinate for 1 hour.

GARNISH AND SERVE THE SALAD | Divide the greens among 4 chilled salad plates. Mound the artichoke mixture in the center of the greens and garnish with the cheese and parsley. Serve immediately.

SERVES 4 AS A FIRST COURSE

Spicy Vegetable Sauté with Cucumber Raita and Beet Chutney

> Steaming the vegetables first and sautéing them just before serving cuts down on the amount of oil needed, while still retaining the textures and flavors of the vegetables. Saffron-flavored rice and crisp flatbread are good accompaniments.

3 cups broccoli florets

1½ cups cauliflower florets

¾ cup diced rutabaga

¾ cup thickly sliced carrots

2 teaspoons vegetable oil

1 tablespoon mustard seeds

1½ teaspoons black onion seeds

1½ teaspoons cumin seeds

⅓ cup diced onion

2 tablespoons minced fresh ginger

2 tablespoons minced jalapeño chile

2 tablespoons minced garlic

4 small dried red chiles

Cucumber Raita (recipe follows)

Beet Chutney (recipe follows)

PREPARE THE VEGETABLES | Steam the broccoli, cauliflower, rutabaga, and carrots separately until each is barely tender. Refrigerate the steamed vegetables until needed.

SAUTÉ THE VEGETABLES WITH THE SPICES | When ready to serve, heat the oil in a large wok or sauté pan over medium-high heat and add the mustard seeds, onion seeds, and cumin seeds. When the seeds begin to pop, add the reserved broccoli, cauliflower, rutabaga, and carrots, and the diced onion, and sauté until the vegetables are heated through, about 3 minutes. Add the ginger, jalapeño, garlic, and dried chiles and sauté for 5 minutes; discard the dried chiles.

GARNISH AND SERVE THE DISH | Serve the vegetables garnished with the Cucumber Raita and Beet Chutney.

SERVES 4 AS A MAIN COURSE

Cucumber Raita

1 cup nonfat plain yogurt

½ cup finely diced English cucumber

Pour the yogurt into a small-holed strainer set over a bowl. Cover the bowl with plastic wrap and place in the refrigerator to drain overnight. Discard the liquid in the bowl and combine the yogurt and cucumber. Refrigerate until needed.

➤ CHEF'S TIP

In India, raitas are served as accompaniments to spicy dishes to act as cooling counterpoints.

Beet Chutney

Vegetable oil spray

10 ounces fresh beets, scrubbed

1 tablespoon red wine vinegar

½ tablespoon minced fresh ginger

1½ teaspoons vegetable oil

1½ teaspoons chopped fresh cilantro

½ tablespoon minced jalapeño chile

¾ teaspoon fresh lime juice

Pinch of cayenne pepper

Preheat the oven to 450°F. Lightly coat a baking pan or cast iron skillet with vegetable oil spray and place the beets in a single layer in the pan. Roast the beets in the oven until tender, about 1 to 1½ hours. Shake the pan every 20 minutes to prevent the beets from sticking or burning. When cool enough to handle, peel the beets and cut them into small dice (wear gloves to prevent staining your hands). Place the beets in a glass or stainless steel bowl and mix them with the vinegar, ginger, oil, cilantro, jalapeño, lime juice, and cayenne. Refrigerate the chutney until needed, up to 1 day ahead of time.

Prosciutto with Grilled Vegetables

A variety of other vegetables can be substituted for those in the recipe. Tender vegetables, such as eggplant, bell peppers, and tomatoes, can be grilled raw if sliced about ¼-inch thick. Denser vegetables, such as fennel, sweet potatoes, and leeks, may burn before cooking fully; parcooking or blanching is necessary before grilling these types of vegetables.

1 head Belgian endive, *quartered*

1 Vidalia onion, cut into ¼-inch-thick slices

1 yellow squash, cut on the diagonal into ¼-inch-thick slices

1 zucchini, cut on the diagonal into ¼-inch-thick slices

1 ounce fresh shiitake mushrooms, stems removed, caps wiped clean

½ pound asparagus, trimmed and peeled

½ bunch green onions, cut into 3½-inch pieces

½ cup homemade or purchased balsamic vinaigrette

1 red bell pepper

1 green bell pepper

1 yellow bell pepper

1 bunch arugula, well washed and dried

3 ounces prosciutto, thinly sliced

1 ounce dry Jack or Parmesan cheese, shaved (see Chef's Tip)

MARINATE THE VEGETABLES | Place the endive, onion, yellow squash, zucchini, mushrooms, asparagus, and green onions in a large bowl. Add ¼ cup of the vinaigrette, toss well, and let the vegetables stand for 30 minutes.

ROAST THE PEPPERS | Preheat a charcoal or gas grill to medium-high (see page 41). Place the bell peppers on the grill and cook until they are charred on all sides. You can also char the peppers under a broiler. Transfer the peppers to a bowl, cover the bowl with plastic wrap, and let the peppers steam until cool enough to handle. Peel the charred skins from the peppers, remove the seeds, and cut them into 2-inch pieces.

GRILL THE VEGETABLES | Grill the remaining vegetables until tender, turning as necessary. The endive will take about 8 minutes; the onion about 5 to 6 minutes; the yellow squash and zucchini about 4 minutes; the mushrooms about 4 minutes; the asparagus about 3 minutes; and the green onions about 2 minutes. Cool the vegetables to room temperature.

GARNISH AND SERVE THE DISH | Divide the arugula among 4 small plates. Scatter the grilled vegetables and roasted peppers over the arugula, dividing evenly. Arrange the prosciutto over the vegetables, dividing evenly, and drizzle each plate with 1 tablespoon of the vinaigrette. Garnish servings with the shaved cheese and serve immediately.

SERVES 4 AS AN APPETIZER

➤ **CHEF'S TIP**
To shave the cheese, draw a sharp vegetable peeler down the length of the cheese, making thin cheese "curls." This technique also works with chocolate for garnishing desserts.

Seared Salmon with Corn, Potato, and Arugula Salad

Using a nonstick skillet, salmon fillets are quickly seared and finished in the oven for a caramelized exterior and moist interior without adding any surplus fat. This makes a perfect entrée for an alfresco summer party.

4 skinless salmon fillets (about 3 ½ ounces each)

¼ teaspoon salt

¼ teaspoon freshly ground black pepper

Corn, Potato, and Arugula Salad (recipe follows)

2 teaspoons chopped fresh chives

2 teaspoons chopped fresh parsley

2 teaspoons chopped fresh chervil

Yellow Tomato Coulis (recipe follows)

10 cherry tomatoes, cut in half

COOK THE SALMON | Preheat the oven to 325°F. Heat a large nonstick ovenproof skillet over medium-high heat. Season the salmon fillets with the salt and pepper. Place the salmon in the pan with the nicest-looking side down and cook until golden brown. Turn the fillets over and place the pan in the oven. Bake the salmon until it is cooked through, about 6 to 8 minutes.

GARNISH AND SERVE THE DISH | Divide the salad among 4 warmed dinner plates, mounding the salad in the center of the plates. Sprinkle the salad with the chopped herbs. Place the salmon fillets on top of the salad. Pour about ¼ cup of the coulis around the salad on each plate and garnish with the cherry tomatoes.

SERVES 4

Corn, Potato, and Arugula Salad

10 ounces red potatoes

1½ tablespoons fresh lemon juice

2 teaspoons fresh lime juice

2½ teaspoons sugar

1½ teaspoons Dijon-style mustard

2 tablespoons peanut oil

1 tablespoon extra-virgin olive oil

1½ cups corn kernels, cooked

½ bunch arugula, well washed and dried

1 tablespoon chopped fresh cilantro

¼ teaspoon salt

Pinch of freshly ground black pepper

Dash of Tabasco sauce

Cook the potatoes in boiling salted water until tender, about 20 minutes. Drain the potatoes and cool slightly. Cut the potatoes into ¼-inch-thick slices. In a small bowl, combine the juices, sugar, and mustard. While whisking, slowly drizzle in the oils until blended. In a serving bowl, combine the corn, potatoes, arugula, and cilantro. Add the juice mixture and toss well. Taste the salad and season with salt, pepper, and Tabasco.

Yellow Tomato Coulis

½ teaspoon olive oil

¼ cup minced onion

1 teaspoon minced garlic

1½ pounds yellow tomatoes, quartered

¾ teaspoon sugar

¼ teaspoon salt

Dash of Tabasco sauce

1 bay leaf

In a large skillet, heat the oil over medium heat. Add the onion and garlic and sauté until the onion is translucent. Add the tomatoes, sugar, salt, Tabasco, and bay leaf, and simmer until the mixture appears dry, about 30 minutes. Remove the bay leaf and process the mixture in a blender until smooth. Strain the coulis through a wire mesh sieve and keep warm.

Fedelini with Broccoli Rabe, Pancetta, and Toasted Bread Crumbs

Pasta with toasted bread crumbs is a popular dish in Italy. Rather that sautéing the bread crumbs in butter or oil, here they are sprayed lightly with olive oil and baked in the oven until golden brown.

½ loaf country white bread

Olive oil spray

1 tablespoon cornstarch

2½ cups chicken broth

⅓ cup evaporated skim milk

2 ounces pancetta, cut into julienne (see Chef's Tip, page 85)

¾ cup diced onion

1½ tablespoons minced garlic

1 pound broccoli rabe, chopped

2 teaspoons chopped fresh thyme

2 teaspoons red pepper flakes

1 tablespoon fresh lemon juice

Salt and freshly ground white pepper to taste

¾ pound dried fedelini or thin spaghetti

⅓ cup freshly grated Parmesan cheese

3 tablespoons chopped fresh Italian parsley

MAKE THE TOASTED BREAD CRUMBS | Preheat the oven to 350°F. Remove the crust from the bread and discard. Cut the bread into large dice and process it in a food processor to medium-sized crumbs. Spread the crumbs on a baking sheet and spray them with the olive oil spray. Bake the crumbs until golden brown, turning frequently; set aside to cool.

MAKE THE SAUCE | In a small bowl or cup, mix the cornstarch with 2 tablespoons of the broth. Bring the remaining broth to a simmer in a small saucepan. Add the cornstarch mixture and the evaporated milk to the simmering broth, stirring constantly until slightly thickened. Keep the sauce warm.

SAUTE THE BROCCOLI RABE WITH THE FLAVORINGS | Preheat a large skillet or wok over medium heat. Add the pancetta and sauté until crisp and browned, about 5 minutes. Add the onion and garlic and sauté until the onion is translucent. Add the broccoli rabe, thyme, and red pepper flakes, and sauté until the broccoli rabe is tender, about 15 minutes. Stir in the broth mixture and simmer until it is reduced to a sauce consistency. Taste and season with the lemon juice, salt, and pepper.

COOK THE PASTA AND COMBINE WITH THE VEGETABLES | Meanwhile, cook the pasta in a large pot of boiling salted water until slightly firm to the bite, *al dente*. Drain the pasta well and add it to the broccoli rabe mixture, tossing the ingredients together well.

GARNISH AND SERVE THE DISH | Divide the pasta mixture among 4 warm serving plates and sprinkle each serving with toasted bread crumbs, Parmesan, and parsley.

SERVES 4

Lemon Tart

The pastry crust for this recipe is leavened with baking powder rather than layers of butter for a lighter texture than with regular pastry crusts. Be sure to use fresh lemon juice to achieve the right tangy flavor.

CRUST

¾ cup plus 2½ tablespoons self-rising flour

¼ teaspoon baking powder

¼ cup plus 1½ teaspoons sugar

1 egg

½ teaspoon grated lemon zest

¼ teaspoon vanilla extract

1 tablespoon canola oil

FILLING

3 tablespoons water

1 teaspoon granulated plain gelatin

1½ cups lemon juice

1½ cups sugar

1½ tablespoons grated lemon zest

4 eggs

2 teaspoons vanilla extract

MAKE THE CRUST | In a food processor or by hand, mix together the flour and baking powder. Add the sugar, egg, lemon zest, and vanilla and mix until blended. Mix in the oil. Add the dry ingredients to the egg mixture and mix until just combined. Cover the dough and refrigerate for at least 20 minutes.

LINE THE TART PAN AND BLIND BAKE THE CRUST | Preheat the oven to 425°F. Press the dough on the bottom and up the sides of a 9-inch fluted tart pan with a removable bottom. Prick the bottom with a fork, line the crust with foil, and weigh it down with dried beans or pie weights. Bake the crust until golden brown, about 12 minutes. Cool completely.

SOFTEN THE GELATIN | Place the water in a small dish and sprinkle with the gelatin; set aside for 5 minutes. Heat the gelatin mixture in a double boiler over simmering water or in a microwave on high (100%) power for 10 to 15 seconds.

MAKE THE LEMON CURD BASE | In a small saucepan, combine the lemon juice, sugar, and lemon zest and bring to a simmer over medium heat. In a bowl, beat the eggs, then quickly stir about one-third of the lemon mixture into the eggs. Whisk the egg-lemon mixture into the remaining lemon mixture in the saucepan and heat, whisking constantly, until the mixture starts to simmer very gently and begins to thicken.

COMBINE THE BASE WITH THE FLAVORING AND GELATIN | Strain the egg-lemon mixture through a fine-meshed sieve into a bowl and stir in the vanilla and melted gelatin. Cool the mixture to room temperature.

ASSEMBLE, CHILL, AND SERVE THE TART | Pour the lemon curd evenly into the crust and smooth the surface. Cover the tart and chill it for several hours or overnight before serving. Cut into wedges to serve.

SERVES 8

Carrot Cake

For this cake, some of the eggs and oil are replaced with egg whites and fruit puree. It's moist and delicious enough to skip the typical cream cheese frosting and present it with a dusting of confectioners' sugar.

Vegetable oil spray

½ cup plus 2 tablespoons all-purpose flour, plus more for dusting the pan

½ cup plus 2 tablespoons whole wheat flour

1 teaspoon baking soda

1 teaspoon baking powder

1 teaspoon ground cinnamon

1 cup plus 2 tablespoons granulated sugar

½ cup vegetable oil

2 eggs

1 pound carrots, peeled and grated

1 cup diced pineapple

⅔ cup raisins

2 egg whites

⅔ cup confectioners' sugar

PREPARE THE CAKE PAN | Preheat the oven to 350°F. Line the bottom of a 10-inch cake pan with parchment or waxed paper. Lightly spray all sides of the pan with vegetable oil spray and dust with flour; set aside.

PREPARE THE CAKE BASE | Into a small bowl, sift the flours, baking soda, baking powder, and cinnamon. In a large bowl, beat the sugar, vegetable oil, and eggs until smooth. Add the dry ingredients to the egg mixture and stir until just blended. Stir in the carrots, pineapple, and raisins.

LIGHTEN THE CAKE BASE WITH EGG WHITES | In a clean, oil-free bowl, whip the egg whites with a mixer or by hand until medium peaks form. Stir one-third of the whites into the cake base. Then, gently fold in the remaining whites until they are incorporated.

BAKE THE CAKE | Pour the cake batter into the prepared pan and bake until a toothpick inserted in the center of the cake comes out clean, about 40 minutes. Cool the cake completely on a rack.

GARNISH AND SERVE THE CAKE | Sift the confectioners' sugar over the cake and cut it into wedges to serve.

SERVES 16

➤ CHEF'S TIPS

To save prep time, you can grate the carrots with a large-holed grating disk of a food processor.

You can also use a decorative pan to bake this cake. Be sure to grease and flour any grooves or impressions well to preserve the presentation.

Individual Chocolate Custards

For these elegant portion-sized custards, nonfat milk replaces much of the cream, and the eggs are lightened with an egg white. Dutch cocoa powder adds rich chocolate flavor with little extra fat.

Vegetable oil spray

2 cups nonfat (skim) milk

1 tablespoon heavy cream

4 tablespoons sugar

½ vanilla bean, split lengthwise

1 egg

1 egg white

1½ ounces semisweet chocolate, chopped

1½ tablespoons Dutch cocoa powder, sifted

Shaved white chocolate or whipped cream for garnish (optional)

PREPARE THE BAKING DISHES | Lightly spray four 6-ounce ramekins with vegetable oil spray. Preheat the oven to 325°F.

INFUSE THE LIQUIDS WITH THE FLAVORINGS | In a medium saucepan, combine the milk, cream, and 2 tablespoons of the sugar. With a paring knife, scrape the seeds from the vanilla bean into the mixture. Bring the mixture just to a boil and remove it from the heat.

PREPARE THE CUSTARD BASE | Meanwhile, whisk together the egg, egg white, and the remaining 2 tablespoons of the sugar in a medium stainless steel bowl; set aside.

MELT THE CHOCOLATE AND COMBINE WITH THE LIQUIDS | Place the chocolate in the top of a double boiler and melt it over hot water. Stir in the cocoa powder. Strain the hot milk mixture through a fine-meshed sieve into the melted chocolate mixture and stir well. Whisk about one-third of the chocolate-milk mixture into the egg mixture; then, whisk the egg mixture back into the remaining chocolate-milk mixture.

BAKE THE CUSTARDS IN A WATER BATH | Pour the chocolate mixture into the prepared ramekins, dividing evenly. Place the ramekins in a baking pan and pour in enough boiling water to come halfway up the sides of the ramekins. Cover the ramekins with waxed paper and bake until the custards are set, about 20 to 30 minutes.

CHILL AND SERVE THE CUSTARDS | Remove the custards from the water bath and refrigerate until thoroughly chilled, 3 to 6 hours, before serving. Garnish with shaved chocolate or whipped cream, if desired.

SERVES 4

Vegetarian

The concept of vegetarianism has become increasingly hard to categorize as it gains a foothold throughout the population. For this section we define vegetarian cooking broadly, excluding red meat, poultry, and fish, but including eggs, cheese and other dairy products.

While we at the CIA believe that all foods are good foods when eaten in moderation, we realize that eating in the vegetarian style, occasionally or regularly, is a sound way to maintain a healthy lifestyle.

These dishes, as in the other chapters, are influenced by a variety of cultures. We've included a few optional ingredients for those who want to change the flavor a bit without retaining the dish's vegetarian qualities.

Wilted Curly Endive and Romaine Salad with Millet Cakes

Millet, a staple grain in many countries of the world, is rich in protein. It is used like rice in a variety of different dishes, and is a common ingredient in multi-grain breads. Here it appears in small sautéed skillet cakes to accompany a wilted greens salad.

MILLET CAKES

¾ cup millet seeds

1 cup milk, lukewarm

Salt and freshly ground black pepper to taste

1 to 2 tablespoons flour

2 large egg whites or 1 whole egg

1 teaspoon chopped fresh herbs

4 teaspoons olive oil

½ cup plus 3 tablespoons olive oil

1 head romaine lettuce, quartered

1 head curly endive, quartered

Salt and freshly ground black pepper to taste

¼ cup finely diced shallots

1 carrot, cut into small dice

½ cup small diced leeks, white part only

¼ cup small diced celery

1 cup balsamic vinegar

¼ cup port wine

Juice from 2 oranges

Chopped fresh chives for garnish

Grated carrots for garnish

PREPARE THE MILLET CAKES | In a saucepan, combine the millet seeds, milk, salt, and pepper and bring to a boil. Stir in 1 tablespoon of the flour and remove the saucepan from the heat; cool. Add the egg whites or egg and the fresh herbs and mix well; the mixture should be the consistency of a thick batter (add more flour if needed). In a large skillet, heat the oil over medium-high heat. Ladle or spoon the batter into the pan in 4 portions. Sauté the cakes until they are golden brown on both sides, adjusting the heat if necessary to avoid scorching the millet seeds. Keep the millet cakes warm in a low oven.

WILT THE LETTUCE | In a large skillet, heat 3 tablespoons of the oil over medium-high heat. If necessary, trim the romaine and endive to fit the size of the pan. Season the lettuces with salt and pepper and sauté for 2 to 3 minutes, until wilted; transfer the lettuces to a plate.

MAKE THE DRESSING | Add the shallots, carrot, leeks, and celery to the skillet and sauté for 2 to 3 minutes. Add the vinegar, port wine, and orange juice and cook until the liquid is reduced by half; cool. Whisk in the remaining ½ cup olive oil, and season with salt and pepper.

ASSEMBLE AND SERVE THE DISH | Arrange the romaine and curly endive on each of 4 warm serving plates. Spoon the dressing over the salad and serve with the millet cakes. Garnish the plates with the chives and grated carrots.

SERVES 4

Barley Salad with Cucumbers and Mint

Nutritious pearl barley replaces bulgur wheat in this tabbouleh salad spin-off. The abundance of fresh parsley, mint, and green onions adds vibrant color and fresh flavor to the salad.

1 pound pearl barley

2 cups peeled, seeded diced tomatoes (see Chef's Tip, page 8)

2 cups diced, peeled and seeded cucumber

2½ cups chopped fresh Italian parsley (about 2 bunches)

½ cup chopped fresh mint

¼ cup finely sliced green onions, white part only

1 cup extra-virgin olive oil

½ cup fresh lemon juice

Salt and freshly ground black pepper to taste

SOAK AND COOK THE BARLEY | Place the barley in a bowl and cover with cold water. Let it stand for 30 minutes and drain well. Place the barley in a saucepan, cover it with salted water, and bring it to a boil over high heat. Reduce the heat to low and simmer until tender, about 40 to 50 minutes; drain the barley and rinse with cold water. Once cooled, drain the barley thoroughly.

ASSEMBLE THE SALAD | Place the barley in a large mixing bowl with the tomatoes, cucumber, parsley, mint, and green onions. In another bowl, whisk together the olive oil, lemon juice, salt, and pepper. Pour the oil mixture over the salad and toss to coat the ingredients evenly. Serve immediately or chill until serving time.

SERVES 10

White Grape Gazpacho with Toasted Almonds and Dill

White grapes are a surprising ingredient in this refreshing cold soup. Cream cheese gives the soup a little more body than would sour cream. English, or hothouse, cucumbers have fewer seeds than regular cucumbers and have a less bitter flavor.

2 pounds white seedless grapes, cut in half

1 English cucumber, diced (do not peel)

4 green onions, green parts only

2 ounces cream cheese

2½ cups half-and-half

2 tablespoons white wine vinegar

1¼ cups plain yogurt

2 tablespoons olive oil

½ cup plus 2 tablespoons chopped fresh dill

Salt and freshly ground white pepper to taste

12 grapes, peeled and halved

¼ cup sliced almonds, toasted

PUREE THE SOUP | In a food processor, combine the 2 pounds grapes, the cucumber, green onions, cream cheese, half-and-half, vinegar, yogurt, olive oil, and ½ cup of the dill. Process the ingredients until smooth. Taste the soup and season with salt and pepper.

GARNISH AND SERVE THE SOUP | Ladle the soup into chilled soup bowls and garnish servings with the remaining chopped dill, the peeled grape halves, and the almonds.

SERVES 8

Rotolo with Mushroom Sauce

You'll love this fresh take on lasagna—the noodles are rolled around, rather than layered with, the rich cheese filling. A savory mushroom, tomato, and fresh herb combination forms the sauce.

¼ cup olive oil

¾ cup minced onion

¾ cup sliced mushrooms
(see Chef's Tip)

1 cup dry red wine

2 cups drained, diced canned plum tomatoes

2 tablespoons minced fresh marjoram

1 teaspoon minced fresh thyme

Salt and freshly ground black pepper to taste

1 pound dry lasagna noodles

1 pound ricotta cheese

1 cup freshly grated Parmesan cheese

1 pound fontina cheese, grated

MAKE THE MUSHROOM SAUCE | In a skillet, heat the olive oil over medium-high heat. Add the onion and sauté until translucent, about 10 to 12 minutes. Add the mushrooms and sauté until the mushrooms are tender, about 8 to 10 minutes. Add the wine and cook over high heat until the wine is reduced by half. Add the tomatoes and herbs, reduce the heat slightly, and simmer until the sauce has a good consistency, about 15 minutes. Taste the sauce and season with salt and pepper.

COOK THE NOODLES | While the sauce is simmering, cook the lasagna noodles in a large pot of boiling salted water until tender, about 12 minutes. Drain the noodles thoroughly, rinse with cold water, and drain again.

FILL THE PASTA ROLLS | Preheat the oven to 400°F. In a bowl, mix together the ricotta and Parmesan cheeses and season the mixture with salt and pepper. Lay the noodles flat on a work surface and spread each noodle with about 1 tablespoon of the ricotta mixture. Scatter about 1 tablespoon of the fontina cheese over each portion of the ricotta mixture. Roll up the noodles around the filling and lay seam-side down in a baking dish.

BAKE THE PASTA ROLLS | Ladle the mushroom sauce over the noodles and bake them for about 30 minutes, or until the dish is very hot and bubbly. Let the dish stand for 10 minutes before serving.

SERVES 7

➤ CHEF'S TIPS

For intense mushroom flavor, use a combination of mushrooms, such as white, brown (cremini), shiitake, oyster, and chanterelle.

For a pasta dish with meat, sprinkle ½ pound thinly sliced prosciutto over the ricotta cheese before rolling up the noodles.

Soba Noodle Salad

An essential ingredient in Japanese cuisine, soba noodles are made from a combination of buckwheat and wheat. In Japan, soba comprises the basis for many different hot and cold dishes; here it's used to make a unique pasta salad.

¼ cup vegetable broth or *dashi* (see Chef's Tips)

2 tablespoons tamari soy sauce

¼ cup rice vinegar

1 tablespoon sugar

1 teaspoon Asian sesame oil

1 tablespoon light miso (see Chef's Tips)

7 ounces thin dried soba noodles

½ cup julienned peeled daikon radish

1 cup radish sprouts

1 medium onion, sliced

2 tablespoons chopped green onions

1 tablespoon sesame seeds, toasted

1 tablespoon Japanese seven-spice powder (see Chef's Tips)

MAKE THE DRESSING | In a bowl, whisk together the broth or dashi, tamari, vinegar, sugar, sesame oil, and miso; set aside.

COOK THE SOBA NOODLES | In a large pot, bring 2 quarts of water to a boil over high heat. Separate the noodles, stir them into the water, and bring the water back to a boil. When the water begins to boil over, add 1 cup of cold water. Repeat the process of boiling and adding cold water two more times. Reduce the heat to low and simmer the noodles until they are tender, about 2 to 3 minutes. Drain the noodles well and plunge them into cold water. Rub the noodles with your hands to remove all of the surface starch. Drain the noodles well.

TOSS THE SALAD | Place the drained noodles in a large bowl. Add the daikon, sprouts, onion, green onions, sesame seeds, and seven-spice powder and toss lightly. Pour the dressing over the salad and toss until the ingredients are coated. Divide the salad among 4 serving plates. Serve immediately.

SERVES 4

➤ CHEF'S TIPS

Dashi is Japanese fish stock, which can be found in liquid or powdered form. Miso, or fermented soybean paste, comes in several different forms, but for this recipe choose the yellow-colored "light" variety. Japanese seven-spice powder is a bold mixture of chiles, sesame seeds, dried orange peel, and other spices; to be authentic, look for the name "shichimi togarashi" on the label. Look for all of these ingredients, including soba noodles, in a Japanese market.

Shaker Potato and Mushroom Stew

This hearty vegetarian stew utilizes meaty mushrooms and sturdy root vegetables as its base. Like a shepherd's pie, pureed potatoes are spread over the stew and the dish is baked until piping hot and browned on the top.

4 bulbs garlic

3 tablespoons olive oil

1½ pounds small white mushrooms

2 pounds oyster mushrooms

3 ounces dried morels

2 quarts vegetable broth or water, warm

10 small shallots, sliced

4 bunches green onions, white and green parts, sliced

12 cloves garlic, minced

3 quarts vegetable broth

2 pounds Yellow Finn or Yukon gold potatoes, cut into large dice

2 pounds Jerusalem artichokes, cut into large dice

1 pound carrots, cut into large dice

Salt and freshly ground black pepper to taste

3 bunches fresh chives, minced

ROAST THE GARLIC | Preheat the oven to 350°F. Slice the tops off the garlic bulbs, exposing the cloves. Place the bulbs on a large sheet of aluminum foil, drizzle them with 2 tablespoons of the oil, and wrap them tightly in the foil. Bake the garlic for about 45 minutes, until soft. When cool enough to handle, squeeze the garlic from the skins into a bowl and set aside.

PREPARE THE MUSHROOMS | Wipe or brush the fresh mushrooms to clean them. Trim the stems to remove just the brown ends. Depending on the shape of the mushroom, or individual preference, slice, halve, quarter, or leave the white mushrooms whole; try to keep the mushroom pieces the same size to ensure even cooking. Soak the morels in the warm broth for 30 minutes, or until softened. Remove the softened morels with a slotted spoon. Strain and reserve the broth.

SAUTÉ THE VEGETABLES | In a flameproof casserole or Dutch oven, heat the remaining 1 tablespoon of the oil over high heat. Add the fresh and dried mushrooms to the pan and sauté until the mushrooms are lightly browned, about 15 minutes. Reduce the heat to medium-high, and add the shallots, green onions, and minced garlic. Sauté for about 3 minutes.

SIMMER THE STEW | Add the 3 quarts broth and bring to a boil over high heat. Reduce the heat to medium and simmer for 20 minutes, skimming the surface as needed. Add the diced potatoes, Jerusalem artichokes, and carrots and simmer the stew, stirring occasionally, until all of the ingredients are very tender, about 15 to 20 minutes. Taste the stew and season with salt and pepper. Reserve 2 tablespoons of the chives. Stir the remaining chives, the parsley, and marjoram into the stew.

1 bunch fresh Italian parsley, minced

2 bunches fresh marjoram, minced

3 pounds russet potatoes, peeled and quartered

Shaker Salad (recipe on page 146) *as accompaniment*

MAKE THE POTATO PUREE | Simmer the russet potatoes in the reserved morel-soaking liquid until very tender, about 25 to 30 minutes; drain the potatoes, reserving the cooking liquid. With a mixer, potato masher, or food mill, mash together the potatoes and reserved garlic until smooth. If necessary, stir in a small amount of the reserved cooking liquid to adjust the consistency (the mixture should hold its shape but be easy to stir and spoon onto plates). Taste the puree and season with salt and pepper. Stir in the reserved 2 tablespoons chives.

ASSEMBLE AND SERVE THE DISH | Preheat the oven to 400°F. Ladle the mushroom mixture into a baking dish or shallow casserole. Spread or pipe the potato puree on top. Bake the stew until it is hot and bubbly and the potatoes have begun to brown, about 20 minutes. Serve portions in soup bowls accompanied by the Shaker Salad.

SERVES 8

Shaker Salad

Fresh herbs and dry mustard enliven this green bean and lettuce salad. The dressing, using thickened broth to replace some of the oil, is a healthy and delicious way to dress any salad.

1¼ cups vegetable broth

1 tablespoon cornstarch, dissolved in a small amount of water

3 tablespoons tarragon vinegar

2 tablespoons minced onion

1 tablespoon minced fresh thyme

2 tablespoons minced fresh savory

¼ cup minced fresh Italian parsley

½ teaspoon dry mustard

Salt and freshly ground black pepper to taste

2 tablespoons olive oil

1 pound green beans, trimmed

2 heads Boston lettuce, torn into bite-sized pieces

3 bunches green onions, thinly sliced

MAKE THE DRESSING | In a saucepan, bring the broth to a simmer over medium heat and add the dissolved cornstarch. Return the broth to a simmer and cook, stirring, for 2 minutes, or until thickened. Remove the broth from the heat and pour it into a bowl. When the broth has cooled to room temperature, add the vinegar, onion, thyme, savory, parsley, mustard, salt, and pepper and whisk until combined. Slowly whisk in the oil. Taste the dressing and adjust the salt and pepper if necessary. The dressing can be prepared up to 24 hours in advance; refrigerate it until you are ready to dress the salad.

COOK THE BEANS | Cut the green beans in half on the bias. Cook the green beans in boiling salted water until tender, about 4 to 5 minutes. Drain the beans and submerge them in ice water until they are chilled. Drain the beans thoroughly.

ASSEMBLE THE SALAD | Place the green beans, lettuce, and green onions in a bowl. Add the whisked dressing and toss until the ingredients are evenly coated. Serve the salad directly from the salad bowl or place on chilled plates.

SERVES 8

Spicy Eggplant, Tomato, and Pepper Casserole

This vegetarian casserole contains a garden of vegetables flavored with Asian ingredients. As the vegetables cook, their nutritious juices are released, then thickened with cornstarch to mingle with the flavorful sauce.

Olive or vegetable oil

3 medium eggplants, peeled and cut into ½-inch-thick slices

1 zucchini, cut into ½-inch-thick slices

1 red bell pepper, seeded, ribs removed, and finely diced

1 green bell pepper, seeded, ribs removed, and finely diced

2 tomatoes, cut into ½-inch-thick slices

1 tablespoon chopped green onions

⅓ cup sesame oil, plus more for sprinkling

1 teaspoon minced garlic

1 teaspoon minced fresh ginger

1 tablespoon hot bean paste (see Chef's Tip)

¾ cup rice vinegar

½ cup sugar

½ cup soy sauce

½ cup sherry

½ cup vegetable broth

1 tablespoon cornstarch, dissolved in water

Hot cooked white rice for accompaniment

SAUTÉ THE VEGETABLES | In a large skillet, heat a small amount of oil over medium-high heat. In batches, add the eggplant slices and sauté for 1 minute on each side, adding more oil as necessary. Drain the sautéed eggplant on paper towels; Add the zucchini to the skillet and sauté for 1 minute on each side, adding more oil if necessary, and drain on paper towels. Add the bell peppers to the skillet and sauté for 2 minutes, adding more oil if necessary; drain on paper towels.

LAYER THE VEGETABLES IN A CASSEROLE | In a greased casserole, layer half of the eggplant. Top with a layer each of the tomatoes, zucchini, and red and green peppers. Sprinkle with the green onions. Finish with a layer of the remaining eggplant.

MAKE THE SAUCE | Preheat the oven to 400°F. In a skillet, heat the sesame oil over medium heat. Add the garlic and ginger and sauté for 1 minute. Add the hot bean paste, vinegar, sugar, soy sauce, sherry, and broth and simmer for 1 minute. Add the dissolved cornstarch and stir until thickened. Pour the sauce over the eggplant in the casserole. Pierce the eggplant with a fork and sprinkle with a small amount of sesame oil.

BAKE AND SERVE THE CASSEROLE | Place the casserole in the oven and bake for 30 minutes, or until the vegetables are tender. Serve portions on warm plates accompanied by hot white rice.

SERVES 4

> ➤ CHEF'S TIP
Look for hot bean paste in jars in an Asian market or the international food aisle of a well-stocked supermarket.

Baked Sweet Potatoes with Marinated Tofu and Wilted Spinach

> Tofu boasts a high protein content, which makes it a terrific stand-in for meat. You can even marinate it and grill it as you would meat or poultry. "Baking" the sweet potatoes on the grill gives them a hint of smoky flavor.

¾ cup dry red wine

¾ cup port wine

6 tablespoons vegetable broth, well seasoned

1 tablespoon brown sugar

¾ cup balsamic vinegar

½ cup olive oil

Salt and freshly ground black pepper to taste

Four 3-ounce slices extra-firm tofu

4 medium-sized sweet potatoes, scrubbed

2 to 3 tablespoons butter

½ cup sour cream, or to taste

1 ounce horseradish, grated

3 tablespoons diced cucumber

¼ cup chopped olives

2 tablespoons lemon juice

One 10-ounce bag fresh spinach leaves

4 sweet potato chips (optional)

4 teaspoons salmon or Beluga caviar (optional)

MARINATE THE TOFU | Place the red wine and port wine in a saucepan and simmer until reduced by one-third. Add the vegetable broth, brown sugar, and vinegar and bring the mixture to a boil; remove from the heat and cool. Add the oil, salt, pepper, and tofu and let the tofu marinate for 2 hours or overnight (place the dish in the refrigerator if marinating for longer than 2 hours).

BAKE THE SWEET POTATOES | Heat the grill to medium-high (see page 41). Rub the sweet potatoes with the butter and season with salt. Wrap the potatoes in aluminum foil, place on the covered grill, and bake for 45 to 50 minutes, or until soft.

GRILL THE TOFU | After the potatoes are cooked, increase the grill heat to high (see page 41). Remove the tofu from the marinade, reserving the marinade, and place the tofu on the grill. Grill the tofu for 1 to 2 minutes on each side, until it is browned and heated through.

MAKE THE SWEET POTATO FILLING | Remove the foil from the sweet potatoes and cut a large lengthwise slit into the flesh. Let the potatoes stand for 5 minutes to allow some of the steam to escape. Cut off the tops of the potatoes and, with a melon baller or small spoon, scoop out the potato flesh, leaving a small amount of potato on the sides to form a shell. Place the potato flesh in a bowl. Add the sour cream, horseradish, cucumber, olives, and lemon juice, and mix carefully until the ingredients are incorporated. Season the mixture with salt and pepper. Spoon the potato filling back into the shells, dividing it evenly. Top each filled potato with a slice of tofu; keep warm.

PREPARE THE SPINACH | Transfer the reserved marinade to a skillet and bring to a boil. Add the spinach and cook, stirring, until the leaves are wilted, about 1 to 2 minutes.

GARNISH AND SERVE THE DISH | Place one tofu-topped potato in the center of 4 serving plates and garnish with the sweet potato chips and caviar, if using. Surround each potato with the wilted spinach. Serve immediately.

SERVES 4

Holidays

The winter holiday season is the perfect time for entertaining, yet some people are full of anxiety at the prospect of creating a large meal for guests. Following is a collection of recipes that are elegant enough for a holiday fête, yet easy to make—even for the most apprehensive cook. Many of the elements of these dishes can be prepared ahead of time, leaving the host free to spend time with his or her guests.

Potato, Crab, and Cheese Strudel

A tossed green salad is a nice accompaniment to this elegant appetizer strudel, stuffed with potatoes, mushrooms, crabmeat, and Gruyère cheese. A trio of fresh herbs is a perfect finishing touch.

⅓ cup olive oil

1 medium-sized red onion, diced

3 cloves garlic, minced

¼ pound crabmeat, picked over

¼ cup brandy

¼ cup chicken broth

¼ pound small white mushrooms, cleaned and sliced

2 large porcini mushrooms, diced

½ pound fingerling potatoes, cooked, peeled, and sliced (see Chef's Tips)

1 tablespoon chopped fresh basil

1 tablespoon chopped fresh cilantro

½ tablespoon chopped fresh lemon thyme

Salt and freshly cracked black pepper to taste

¼ cup shredded Gruyère cheese

2 egg yolks

8 sheets phyllo pastry (see Chef's Tips)

Clarified butter (ghee) (see Chef's Tip, page 47)

PREPARE THE FILLING | In a large skillet, heat one-half of the oil over medium heat. Add the red onion, garlic, and crabmeat and sauté briefly. Add the brandy, chicken broth, white mushrooms, and porcinis. Simmer slowly for 3 minutes and set aside. In another skillet, heat the remaining oil over medium-high heat. Add the potato slices and sauté until golden brown on both sides. Add the basil, cilantro, thyme, salt, and pepper and mix well. Transfer the potato mixture to the pan with the crab-mushroom mixture and cook until thoroughly heated through; cool. In a bowl, mix the Gruyère cheese with the egg yolks. Add this mixture to the crab mixture and gently fold together until combined.

ASSEMBLE THE STRUDEL | Lay one sheet of phyllo on a clean work surface and brush with clarified butter. Top with two more sheets of phyllo, brushing with butter in between. Top with a fourth sheet of phyllo. Spread the phyllo evenly with half of the filling. Roll the phyllo lengthwise around the filling into a cylindrical shape. Brush the outside of the roll with butter and place on a baking sheet. Repeat the layering, filling, and rolling process with the remaining phyllo and filling. Refrigerate the rolls for 1 hour.

BAKE AND SERVE THE STRUDEL | Preheat the oven to 375°F. Place the rolls on a baking sheet and bake until golden brown on all sides, approximately 6 to 12 minutes. Cool slightly and cut into serving slices.

SERVES 10 AS AN APPETIZER

➤ **CHEF'S TIPS**

Fingerling potatoes are about the size and shape of a large thumb. Look for them in a specialty foods store or farmers' market.

Phyllo pastry dries out very quickly. As you work with each phyllo sheet, keep the remaining sheets covered with plastic wrap or a moist dishtowel at all times.

Brussels Sprouts with Chestnuts

Brussels sprouts, a common addition to the holiday spread, are updated with chestnuts and a hint of caramely brown sugar. Choose sprouts that are evenly sized—ideally on the small side—for the best flavor.

2 pounds Brussels sprouts

1½ cups chicken broth

½ cup shredded chestnuts

Salt and freshly ground black pepper to taste

Light brown sugar to taste

2 tablespoons butter

COOK THE BRUSSELS SPROUTS | Trim the stem ends from the Brussels sprouts and cut an X in the bases. Pull away any loose or wilted leaves. Cook the Brussels sprouts in simmering salted water until tender, about 15 to 20 minutes, depending on the size of the sprouts. Drain thoroughly.

COOK THE CHESTNUTS | In a skillet, bring the chicken broth to a boil and add the shredded chestnuts. Simmer over low heat for 15 minutes, or until the broth is well reduced. Add the salt, pepper, and brown sugar, and continue to simmer until the chestnuts are lightly glazed.

TOSS THE COMPONENTS TOGETHER | Add the Brussels sprouts and butter to the skillet and toss over low heat for 2 minutes, or until all of the ingredients are very hot. Serve immediately.

SERVES 8

Sweet Potato-Stuffed Apples

Here the ubiquitous holiday sweet potato casserole takes an elegant turn. The pureed sweet potatoes are stuffed into tart-sweet apples and topped with marshmallows before baking.

4 medium-sized sweet *potatoes*, scrubbed

2 tablespoons vegetable oil

¼ cup light brown sugar, or to taste

3 tablespoons butter, melted

Salt and freshly ground black pepper to taste

8 Rome apples, or other baking apples, cored

8 marshmallows

PREHEAT THE OVEN TO 400°F.

COOK THE SWEET POTATOES | Lightly rub the sweet potatoes with oil and bake them in the oven until very tender, about 45 to 50 minutes. Remove the potatoes from the oven and reduce the oven heat to 350°F.

PREPARE THE STUFFING | Remove the skin from the sweet potatoes and puree the flesh in a food processor. Place the pureed sweet potato in a bowl with the brown sugar, melted butter, salt, and pepper. Transfer the sweet potato mixture to a pastry bag.

FILL THE APPLES | Pipe the sweet potato mixture into the cored apples, dividing evenly. Press a marshmallow on top of the puree in each apple and place the filled apples in a lightly buttered baking dish. Bake until the apples are tender and the filling is very hot, about 15 to 20 minutes. Serve warm.

SERVES 8

Apple-Brined and Hickory-Smoked Turkey

Brining turkey in a salt and sugar solution before smoking creates succulent, juicy meat for your holiday table. Apple juice, ginger, garlic, and spices are infused into the bird for incredible flavor.

2 quarts apple juice

1 pound brown sugar

1 cup kosher salt

3 quarts water

3 oranges, quartered

4 ounces fresh ginger, thinly sliced

15 whole cloves

6 bay leaves

6 large cloves garlic, crushed

One 12- to 14-pound turkey

Hickory chips, soaked in water for at least 30 minutes

Vegetable oil

PREPARE THE BRINE | In a large saucepan over high heat, bring the apple juice, brown sugar, and salt to a boil, stirring to dissolve the sugar and salt. Cook for 1 minute, remove from the heat, and skim off the foam. Allow the mixture to cool to room temperature. In a 5-gallon plastic bucket or other container large enough to easily hold the turkey, combine the water, oranges, ginger, cloves, bay leaves, and garlic. Add the apple juice mixture and stir.

SOAK THE TURKEY IN THE BRINE | Remove and discard the fat from the turkey cavity. Reserve the neck and giblets for another use. Rinse the turkey inside and out, drain, and submerge the turkey in the brine. If necessary, top with a heavy weight to make sure it is completely immersed. Refrigerate for 24 hours.

PREPARE THE SMOKER | Follow the grill manufacturer's instructions for using wood chips. Set up the grill for indirect cooking over medium heat (see pages 24 and 41).

SMOKE THE TURKEY | Remove the turkey from the brine and pat with paper towels until very dry. Tie the turkey legs together with kitchen string. Lightly brush the turkey with vegetable oil, and place on a roasting rack set inside a heavy-gauge foil pan. Cook the turkey indirectly over medium heat on the covered grill. When the wings are golden brown, about 40 minutes, wrap them with aluminum foil to prevent them from burning. Brush the rest of the turkey with vegetable oil. When the turkey breasts are golden brown, about 1 hour, cover the turkey with aluminum foil to prevent the skin from getting too brown. The turkey is done when its juices run clear, the internal temperature of the thickest part of the thighs is about 180°F, and the internal temperature of the breast is about 170°F; figure about 12 to 14 minutes per pound.

REST AND CARVE THE TURKEY | Transfer the turkey to a cutting board or platter, cover loosely with aluminum foil, and let rest for 20 minutes before carving into serving pieces.

SERVES 12 TO 15

REPRINTED FROM *WEBER'S ART OF THE GRILL*, CHRONICLE BOOKS, 1999

Sausage, Apple, and Walnut Stuffing

Perk up your traditional holiday stuffing with savory sausage, tangy apples, and crunchy walnuts. Baked in a dish rather than inside the bird, it gains a crispy, golden brown exterior.

6 tablespoons butter

½ cup finely diced celery

½ cup finely diced onion

1 cup uncooked hot or mild bulk sausage, crumbled

6 cups cubed white bread

1 cup diced peeled apples

½ cup chopped toasted walnuts

½ cup chicken broth, or as needed

2 tablespoons minced fresh Italian parsley

Salt and freshly ground black pepper to taste

SAUTÉ THE VEGETABLES | In a large skillet, melt the butter over medium heat. Add the celery and onion and sauté for about 10 minutes, until the vegetables are tender. Add the sausage and sauté until the sausage is crumbly and no pink remains. Stir in the bread cubes, tossing them with the other ingredients, and sauté for about 1 minute. Remove the skillet from the heat.

MIX THE REMAINING INGREDIENTS | Transfer the sautéed mixture to a bowl. Add the apples and walnuts and toss the ingredients until mixed. If the stuffing needs additional moisture, add the chicken broth (it should be moist, but not wet). Add the parsley and season generously with salt and pepper.

BAKE THE STUFFING | Preheat the oven to 375°F. Place the stuffing in a baking pan and bake until it is hot throughout and the top is golden brown.

MAKES ABOUT 8 CUPS

Pork Crown Roast

This sophisticated entrée is deceptively easy to prepare. As there are few items in this recipe, select only the best raw ingredients. Visit a reputable butcher for top-quality meat.

One crown roast of pork, about 6 to 7 pounds, trimmed and tied (ask your butcher)

Salt and freshly ground black pepper to taste

4 cloves garlic, cut into slivers

PREPARE THE PORK FOR ROASTING | Preheat the oven to 400°F. Season the pork with salt and pepper. With a paring knife, cut a small slit between each bone and insert a piece of garlic clove. Crimp some aluminum foil around the exposed bones to keep them from scorching as the pork roasts.

ROAST THE PORK | Place the roast on a rack in a roasting pan. Place a ball of crumpled aluminum foil in the center of the roast to keep it from collapsing inward as it cooks. Roast the pork for 15 minutes. Reduce the oven heat to 350°F and continue to roast the pork for 2 hours, or until the internal temperature is 160°F.

REST AND CARVE THE PORK | Remove the pork from the oven, and let it stand on a carving board or large platter for about 15 minutes before carving. To carve the roast, use a slicing knife to cut between each bone.

SERVES 8

Pumpkin Mascarpone Cheesecake

Serve this cake instead of the expected pumpkin pie at your next Thanksgiving or Christmas feast. Italian double-cream mascarpone cheese makes this a true holiday indulgence.

CRUST

1¼ cups graham cracker crumbs

2 tablespoons sugar

2 tablespoons butter, melted

1 teaspoon egg white

PUMPKIN FILLING

1½ pounds cream cheese, at room temperature

1 cup plus 1 tablespoon packed brown sugar

1¾ cups pumpkin puree (homemade or canned)

½ teaspoon ground ginger

¾ teaspoon ground cinnamon

½ teaspoon ground mace

Pinch of salt

9 ounces mascarpone cheese

2 eggs

PREPARE THE CAKE PAN | Preheat the oven to 325°F. Butter the sides and bottom of a 10-inch cake pan and line the bottom with a circle of parchment paper.

MAKE THE CRUST | In a shallow pan, blend the graham cracker crumbs and sugar evenly with a fork. Add the melted butter and egg white and mix well. Press the graham mixture into the prepared cake pan to make an even bottom crust. Bake the crust until it is lightly toasted and set, about 8 minutes. Cool slightly.

MAKE THE PUMPKIN FILLING | In a bowl, combine the cream cheese and brown sugar. With a mixer on low speed, or with a wooden spoon by hand, blend the ingredients until very smooth. Take care not to overbeat the mixture or you will incorporate too much air into the cheesecake. Add the pumpkin puree, ginger, cinnamon, mace, and salt and mix gently for 3 to 4 minutes, scraping down the sides and bottom of the bowl often, until the mixture is evenly blended. Add the mascarpone and mix gently for 2 to 3 minutes, scraping the bowl. Add the eggs and mix for 2 to 3 minutes, scraping the bowl as necessary.

BAKE THE CHEESECAKE | Pour the pumpkin filling over the crust. Place the filled cake pan in a deep baking dish; set this assembly on the oven rack. Add enough boiling water to the baking pan to come two-thirds to three-fourths of the way up the sides of the cake pan. Bake the cake for 1¼ hours, or until the center of the cake is lightly set. Carefully remove the cheesecake from the baking pan and cool it to room temperature. Refrigerate the cake for at least 8 hours before unmolding.

UNMOLD THE CAKE | Carefully lower the cake pan into a pan of hot water for a few seconds. Invert the cake pan onto a plate, then invert the cake onto a serving plate.

SLICE AND SERVE THE CAKE | Dip a sharp knife with a long, thin blade into very hot water. Wipe the blade dry and make a cut. For the neatest slices, repeat this process for each separate cut that is made.

SERVES 10 TO 12

Swan Meringues

Dramatic looking, but simple to make, this dessert is a light, refreshing way to end an indulgent special occasion meal. A bonus for harried cooks: you can prepare all of the elements in advance of the party and assemble them at the last minute.

CANDIED CRANBERRIES

1 ½ cups sugar

1 cup water

1 cup fresh or frozen cranberries

MERINGUE

2 ¼ cups sugar

8 egg whites

½ teaspoon cream of tartar

Crème Anglaise (recipe follows)

Homemade or purchased red fruit sorbet, such as cranberry or raspberry

Grated fresh orange zest for garnish

MAKE THE CANDIED CRANBERRIES | In a saucepan, combine the sugar and water. Bring the mixture to a simmer over medium-high heat and stir to dissolve the sugar. Add the cranberries and simmer for about 15 to 20 minutes, until the cranberries are shiny, plump, and taste very sweet. Strain the cranberries and place them on a rack to dry overnight.

MAKE THE MERINGUE | In a large bowl, combine the sugar, egg whites, and cream of tartar. Beat the mixture over a simmering water bath until it reaches 110°F. Whip with a mixer on high speed until it begins to recede from the sides of the bowl.

PIPE AND BAKE THE MERINGUE SHAPES | Preheat the oven to 225°F. Transfer the meringue to a clean, grease-free piping bag with a plain tip. Pipe the meringue onto a parchment-covered baking sheet into 12 question mark shapes, with a ball at the top to resemble swans' heads. Pipe six 3-inch circles to serve as bases on which the swans will rest. On another parchment-lined baking sheet, trace 12 swans' wings onto the parchment with a pencil; be sure that the wing size is in proportion to the body size. Pipe the meringue onto the traced shapes. Place the baking sheets in the oven and bake for about 1 hour, until the meringues are very dry; take care that the meringues do not turn brown—turn the oven heat down or off if necessary.

ASSEMBLE THE DESSERTS | Spoon about ⅓ cup of the Crème Anglaise onto each of 6 dessert plates. Place one meringue circle in the center of each plate to serve as a base. Top each circle with a large scoop of sorbet. Press 2 swan bodies and 2 swan wings into the sides of each scoop of sorbet. Sprinkle the candied cranberries and orange zest around the swans and serve immediately.

SERVES 6

Crème Anglaise

2 cups heavy cream

1 cup milk

1 vanilla bean, scraped

½ cup sugar

6 large egg yolks

Place the cream, milk, and vanilla bean in a saucepan and bring just to a boil; remove from the heat. In a bowl, combine the sugar and egg yolks and whisk until blended. While whisking, slowly add the hot cream mixture until the ingredients are blended. Return the mixture to the saucepan over low heat and cook, stirring, until the mixture thickens enough to coat the back of a metal spoon. Strain the mixture into a bowl and cool. Refrigerate until ready to serve.

MAKES 2½ CUPS

Sweets

You can find a dessert for any occasion in this chapter. Old-time favorites, chocolate indulgences, and low-fat selections are all here.

Many of these desserts consist of two or more different elements, which can be mixed and matched for ultimate sweet satisfaction. Don't forget to consult the other chapters for their desserts, too.

Lemon-Lime Tart with Marinated Berries and Orange Granite

The lemon-lime curd that fills the tart can also be used as a companion to teatime scones. The marinated summer berries can double as a sauce for ice cream. For an elegant, light dessert, accompany the granite—flavored with Grand Marnier—with a delicate cookie.

TART DOUGH

½ cup sugar

½ cup butter

½ teaspoon vanilla extract

1 teaspoon grated lemon zest

1 egg

3¼ cups pastry flour, sifted

LEMON-LIME CURD

4½ egg yolks

4½ eggs

½ cup sugar

Grated zest of ½ lemon

Grated zest of ½ lime

2 tablespoons plus 1 teaspoon lemon juice

2 tablespoons plus 1 teaspoon fresh lime juice

14 tablespoons butter, cut into cubes

Marinated Berries (recipe follows)

Orange Granite (recipe follows)

PREPARE THE TART DOUGH | In a food processor or by hand, blend the sugar and butter until smooth. Mix in the vanilla extract and the lemon zest. Add the egg slowly and mix it in gently but thoroughly. Add the flour and mix just until incorporated (pulse in short bursts if using a food processor). Wrap the dough in plastic wrap and refrigerate until needed.

BAKE THE CRUST | Preheat the oven to 350°F. On a lightly floured board, roll the tart dough into a circle ⅛-inch thick. Transfer the dough to a 10-inch tart pan with a removable bottom and trim the edges with a paring knife. Line the dough with waxed paper or parchment paper and fill with pie weights or dried beans. Bake the dough for approximately 20 minutes, or until golden brown; set aside to cool.

PREPARE THE LEMON-LIME CURD FILLING | In the top of a double boiler, combine the egg yolks, eggs, sugar, lemon zest, lime zest, lemon juice, and lime juice. Cook over simmering water, whisking constantly with a mixer or by hand, until the mixture reaches 180°F. Remove from the heat. Add the butter a piece at a time and whisk until it is incorporated. Pour the lemon-lime curd into the baked tart shell and refrigerate or freeze until serving time.

GARNISH AND SERVE THE TART | Cut the tart into serving wedges. Serve on dessert plates accompanied by the Marinated Berries and Orange Granite.

SERVES 6

➤ (recipe continues on following page)

Marinated Berries

1 cup sugar

½ cup plus 2 tablespoons water

6 tablespoons corn syrup

3 tablespoons cassis syrup

3 tablespoons Grand Marnier

3 tablespoons grenadine syrup

1 tablespoon fresh lemon juice

18 ounces assorted summer berries

In a saucepan, combine the sugar, water, corn syrup, cassis, Grand Marnier, grenadine, and lemon juice. Heat the mixture until the sugar is dissolved; cool. Place the berries in a bowl and add the marinade. Let them stand for at least 1 hour before serving, stirring occasionally.

SERVES 6

Orange Granite

2 cups fresh orange juice

¾ cup white wine

3 tablespoons Grand Marnier

¼ cup sugar

Grated zest of 1 orange

In a saucepan, combine all of the ingredients and heat over low heat just until the sugar is dissolved. Cool the mixture over an ice bath and pour into a shallow, glass or stainless steel pan. Place the pan in the freezer and freeze overnight. Break the granite into small pieces and chop in a food processor, pulsing the machine in short bursts, until a relatively smooth mixture forms. Serve immediately using a scoop or two spoons to form portions.

MAKES ABOUT 1 QUART

Low-Fat Brownies with Buttermilk Sherbet and Marinated Strawberries

Cocoa powder and egg whites replace the chocolate and some of the eggs, making brownies that are still moist and full flavored, yet low in fat and calories. Buttermilk is naturally low in fat and its distinctive flavor makes a scrumptious frozen treat.

1½ cups all-purpose flour

1 cup unsweetened cocoa powder

½ teaspoon baking powder

½ teaspoon salt

8½ tablespoons butter

1 cup plus 1 tablespoon sugar

1 egg

2 egg whites

1 teaspoon vanilla extract

Buttermilk Sherbet (recipe follows)

Marinated Strawberries (recipe follows)

PREPARE THE BROWNIE BATTER | Preheat the oven to 350°F. Lightly grease a 10-inch cake pan with vegetable oil. Into a bowl, sift the flour, cocoa, baking powder, and salt. In a saucepan, melt the butter. Remove the pan from the heat and stir in the sugar until well blended. In a bowl, beat together the egg, egg whites, and vanilla, and stir this mixture into the sugar mixture. Beat well by hand with a wooden spoon for about 1 minute. Add the combined dry ingredients and continue to stir just until the batter is evenly moistened.

BAKE AND SERVE THE BROWNIES | Pour the batter into the prepared cake pan and bake for about 25 to 30 minutes, or until baked through. Let the brownies cool in the pan. Cut the brownies into serving wedges. Serve the brownies with the Buttermilk Sherbet and Marinated Strawberries.

SERVES 16

Buttermilk Sherbet

4 cups buttermilk

1½ cups light corn syrup

½ cup sugar

1 vanilla bean, split, or
2 teaspoons vanilla extract

½ cup fresh lemon juice

In a glass or stainless steel saucepan, combine the buttermilk, corn syrup, sugar, and vanilla bean, if using. Stir the mixture over low heat just until the sugar dissolves (you will not feel any graininess in the bottom of the pan as you stir). Remove the vanilla bean and reserve for another use. Cool the buttermilk mixture over an ice bath or in the refrigerator. When it is very cold (40°F or less), stir in the vanilla extract, if using, and the lemon juice. Freeze the mixture in an ice cream maker according to the manufacturer's directions. Keep frozen until ready to serve.

MAKES ABOUT 2 QUARTS

Marinated Strawberries

2 cups hulled and quartered strawberries

2 tablespoons sugar

2 tablespoons Grand Marnier

2 tablespoons orange juice

2 tablespoons honey

⅛ teaspoon vanilla extract

1 tablespoon finely chopped fresh mint leaves

In a bowl, combine all of the ingredients and toss gently until evenly blended. Refrigerate the berries for 1 hour before serving, stirring occasionally.

SERVES 16

Fat-Free Chocolate Gelato with Bananas and Honey-Orange Sauce

Indulge your chocolate craving with this rich-tasting gelato, accented by honey- and orange-glazed bananas. The sauce is made quickly in a skillet and the bananas are simmered in it until gently warmed and glazed.

2 cups plus 5 tablespoons water

1½ cups nonfat dry milk powder

⅔ cup unsweetened cocoa powder

¾ cup sugar

1 teaspoon vanilla extract

1 pint orange juice

¼ cup honey

1 vanilla bean, split

10 bananas

½ cup heavy cream

MAKE THE GELATO | In a saucepan, combine the water, nonfat dry milk, cocoa, and sugar. Stir over low heat just until the sugar is dissolved. Stir in the vanilla extract and cool completely. Freeze the gelato in an ice cream maker according to the manufacturer's directions. Store in the freezer until ready to serve.

MAKE THE GLAZED BANANAS | In a stainless steel skillet, combine the orange juice, honey, and vanilla bean, and simmer for 5 minutes. Peel and slice the bananas and add them to the pan with the orange juice mixture. Cook until the bananas are gently warmed through.

GARNISH AND SERVE THE DISH | In a bowl, whip the cream with a mixer or by hand until soft peaks form. Divide the banana slices among 10 serving plates. Place scoops of the gelato in the center of each plate. Ladle a scant ¼ cup of the sauce over the bananas and top with a small dollop of the whipped cream.

SERVES 10

Chocolate Lace Cups with Chocolate Sorbet

For this double-chocolate treat, chocolate wafer cookies are fashioned into a cup that holds a rich chocolate sorbet. If desired, accompany servings with fresh seasonal berries.

CHOCOLATE SORBET

2 cups water

1 cup sugar

1 cup unsweetened cocoa powder

7 ounces semisweet chocolate, finely chopped

CHOCOLATE LACE CUPS

8 tablespoons butter

½ cup plus 2 tablespoons light corn syrup

3 tablespoons brown sugar

½ cup all-purpose flour

2½ tablespoons best-quality unsweetened cocoa powder, such as Valrhona

MAKE THE SORBET | In a saucepan, bring the water and sugar to a boil. Add the cocoa powder and stir until dissolved. Add the chocolate and continue to stir until dissolved. Cool the mixture over an ice bath or in the refrigerator. Freeze in an ice cream maker according to manufacturer's directions and store in the freezer until ready to serve.

MAKE THE CHOCOLATE LACE CUPS | Preheat the oven to 350°F. In a saucepan, melt the butter. Add the corn syrup, sugar, sifted flour, and cocoa powder and mix until incorporated. Chill the mixture until it is firm. Scoop out portions (about 2 tablespoons) and place on a level ungreased sheet pan; spread the dough out to form a 6- to 7-inch diameter circle. Bake for approximately 10 minutes. Cool the cookies slightly, but while still warm, place them onto inverted cups, shaping them with your fingertips for a pleated or ruffled effect, if desired. If the cookies cool too quickly, return them to the oven briefly until pliable. Cool the cookies and store in an airtight container until ready to use.

SERVE THE DESSERT | At serving time, place scoops of the sorbet into the chocolate lace cups and serve immediately.

SERVES 10

Triple Chocolate Mousse Cake with Sour Cherry Sauce

This elegant special occasion cake seems like a lot of work, but its elements can be prepared in advance and assembled at the last minute. You can vary the recipe by baking the cake in a rectangular mold, or other shape of cake pan.

FLOURLESS CHOCOLATE CAKE

10 egg yolks

1 cup sugar

7 egg whites

⅔ cup sugar

1 cup unsweetened cocoa powder, sifted

SOUR CHERRY SAUCE

¾ cup dried cherries

7 tablespoons sugar

1½ cups red wine

½ cup plus 2 tablespoons water

2 tablespoons orange juice

2 tablespoons lemon juice

1 cinnamon stick

➥ (ingredients and recipe continue on following page)

MAKE THE FLOURLESS CHOCOLATE CAKE | One day before serving, preheat the oven to 350°F. Line a 10-inch round cake pan with parchment paper and spray it with vegetable oil spray. With the whip attachment of an electric mixer, whip the egg yolks and sugar on high speed until the mixture is very full in volume and recedes slightly from the highest point that it reached in the bowl. In a clean, oil-free bowl and with a clean whip, whip the egg whites until foamy. Add the sugar and continue to whip until medium-stiff peaks are formed. With a rubber spatula, gently fold the egg white mixture into the yolk mixture until incorporated. Then, fold in the sifted cocoa powder. Pour the batter into the prepared pan and bake for approximately 15 to 18 minutes. Cool completely on a rack. Wrap the cooled cake with plastic wrap.

MAKE THE SOUR CHERRY SAUCE | One day before serving, place the cherries in a heat-proof bowl. In a heavy-bottomed stainless steel saucepan, combine the sugar, red wine, water, orange juice, lemon juice, and cinnamon stick. Bring the mixture to a boil over high heat. Pour the hot liquid over the dried cherries and let stand until cool. Cover the bowl and refrigerate overnight.

PREPARE THE MOUSSE LAYERS | Pour 1½ cups of the heavy cream into a bowl and whip until soft peaks form; reserve in the refrigerator. Place each of the chocolates in a separate bowl. In a saucepan, bring ¼ cup of the heavy cream to a boil with the scraped vanilla bean. Remove and discard the vanilla bean and divide the hot cream among the bowls with the chocolate and stir each mixture until smooth. Reserve each mixture at room temperature. In the top of a double boiler, combine the gelatin and the rum or other liqueur. Place over simmering water until the gelatin reaches approximately 90°F; cool. In another saucepan, bring the remaining ¼ cup of the heavy cream to a boil. In a stainless-steel bowl, beat the egg yolks with the sugar. While whisking, ladle a small amount of the hot cream into the yolks. Then, return the warm yolk mixture to the cream mixture on the stove and cook, stirring, until it coats the back of a metal spoon. Cool the mixture to room temperature.

TRIPLE CHOCOLATE MOUSSE

2¼ cups heavy cream

1½ ounces semisweet chocolate, chopped

1½ ounces milk chocolate, chopped

1½ ounces white chocolate, chopped

⅓ vanilla bean, scraped

1 teaspoon gelatin

1 tablespoon dark rum

¼ cup heavy cream

2 egg yolks

1½ teaspoons sugar

¼ cup dark rum

3 tablespoons red wine

2½ teaspoons cornstarch

Shaved chocolate for garnish

PREPARE THE MOUSSE LAYERS | Add the gelatin mixture to the hot cream and egg yolk mixture and stir until the gelatin is dissolved; then, divide the mixture among the 3 types of chocolate and blend well.

ASSEMBLE THE CAKE | Place the Flourless Chocolate Cake in a clean, lightly oiled springform pan and brush with the dark rum. Fold one-third of the reserved whipped cream into the dark chocolate mousse and spread it in an even layer over the flourless chocolate cake. Chill the cake in the freezer for 15 to 20 minutes. Fold one-third of the whipped cream into the milk chocolate mousse and spread it in an even layer over the dark chocolate mousse; chill in the freezer for 15 to 20 minutes. Fold the remaining cream into the white chocolate mousse and spread it in an even layer over the milk chocolate mousse. Chill the cake in the refrigerator until the mousses are set, at least 3 hours.

FINISH THE SAUCE | Strain the cherries, transferring the soaking liquid to a stainless steel saucepan. Bring the cherry liquid to a boil. In a bowl, mix together the 3 tablespoons of wine and the cornstarch and add this to the boiling liquid, stirring until thickened. Stir in the cherries; set aside until needed.

GARNISH AND SERVE THE DESSERT | To serve, remove the sides of the springform pan. Dip a sharp knife with a long, thin blade into very hot water. Wipe the blade dry and make a cut. For the neatest slices, repeat this process for each separate slice that is made. Spoon a small amount of cherry sauce onto the plates around the cake servings and garnish with shaved chocolate.

SERVES 10

Bananas Foster

This fifties-style dessert hails from New Orleans, where people never skimp on flavor or calories. Though the presentation is elegant, the dessert is surprisingly easy to put together.

2 firm, ripe bananas

3 tablespoons butter

2 tablespoons sugar

½ teaspoon lemon juice

3 tablespoons dark or light rum

1 tablespoon banana liqueur

1 pint good-quality vanilla
ice cream

PREPARE THE SAUCE AND COOK THE BANANAS | Peel the bananas and cut them into rounds, or on the diagonal, into ½-inch-thick slices. In a large skillet, heat the butter over medium-high heat. Add the sugar and cook until the sugar has started to darken slightly. Add the lemon juice and swirl it into the butter mixture. Add the sliced bananas and cook for about 2 to 3 minutes, until the bananas give off a good aroma and have started to soften.

ADD THE LIQUOR | Remove the pan from the heat. Add the rum and banana liqueur to the skillet, return it to the heat, and bring the liquid to a simmer. (If desired, you can ignite the sauce with a long match, but it is not essential. Continue with the recipe when the flames are extinguished.)

SERVE THE DESSERT | Divide scoops of the ice cream among 4 dessert bowls. Ladle the bananas and sauce over the ice cream and serve immediately.

SERVES 4

Orange Chiffon Cake

A piece of cake for dessert need not ruin your diet—just select a recipe that's high in flavor and low in fat. This easy-to-prepare cake, flavored with fresh orange juice and zest, is a good example.

3½ cups cake flour

5¼ teaspoons baking powder

1½ teaspoons salt

2⅔ cups sugar

Scant 1 cup vegetable oil

10 egg yolks

1 cup water

Juice and grated zest of 2 oranges

7 egg whites

Scant ⅔ cup sugar

Pinch of cream of tartar

Confectioners' sugar

PREHEAT THE OVEN TO 350°F. GREASE AND FLOUR TWO 7-INCH TUBE PANS.

PREPARE THE CAKE BASE | Sift together the flour, baking powder, salt, and sugar. Combine the oil, egg yolks, water, orange juice, and zest. Add the liquid ingredients to the dry ingredients blend until smooth.

WHIP AND FOLD IN THE EGG WHITES | In a clean, oil-free bowl, whip the egg whites with a mixer or by hand with the sugar and cream of tartar until medium-soft peaks form. With a rubber spatula, gradually fold the egg whites into the cake base, taking care not to overmix.

BAKE THE CAKES | Pour the batter into the prepared pans and bake for 45 minutes, or until a cake tester inserted into the center of the cakes comes out clean. Remove the pans from the oven, carefully invert the pans, and cool completely.

GARNISH AND SERVE THE CAKES | When cool, release the cakes from the sides of the pan with a spatula and invert onto serving plates. Dust the cakes with confectioners' sugar and cut into serving pieces.

SERVES 12 TO 16

Warm Apple Streusel Tartlets

A crumbly mixture of butter, sugar, flour, and cinnamon tops these individual apple tarts. Walnuts are a surprising addition, adding nutty flavor and crunch to the filling. Dried cranberries or sour cherries could replace the raisins or currants if they suit your fancy.

Tart Dough (see page 163)

2 pounds Granny Smith apples

3½ tablespoons cinnamon sugar see Chef's Tip, page 73)

1 teaspoon all-purpose flour

4 ounces raisins or dried currants

1¼ ounces walnuts, chopped

½ cup butter, softened

⅔ cup sugar

1½ cups flour

Ground cinnamon to taste (optional)

LINE THE TARTLET PANS | Preheat the oven to 375°F. On a lightly floured work surface, roll out the dough until it is ⅛-inch thick. With a 5-inch cutter, cut the dough into eight circles and transfer the pastry circles to eight 4½-inch tartlet pans. Push the dough into the crimps on the edges of the pans.

MAKE THE FILLING | Peel and core the apples and slice into quarters. Cut each quarter crosswise into thin slices. Place the apple slices in a bowl and toss with the cinnamon sugar and flour. Stir in the raisins or currants and walnuts.

MAKE THE STREUSEL TOPPING | In a food processor or by hand, mix the butter and sugar until light and creamy. Add the flour and mix until a rough, crumbly mixture forms (pulse in short bursts if using a food processor). Mix in the cinnamon, if desired; set aside.

FILL THE TARTLETS | Divide the apple mixture among the lined tartlet pans, packing the filling slightly. Sprinkle the tartlets with the streusel mixture, dividing evenly.

BAKE AND SERVE THE TARTLETS | Bake the tartlets for 1 to 1¼ hours, until the apples are cooked, and the streusel is golden brown. Let the tartlets stand at room temperature for 30 minutes before serving. Serve warm.

MAKES EIGHT 4¹⁄₂-INCH TARTLETS

Index

Acknowledgments

Every week, hundreds of people line up both in Hyde Park, New York, and in the Napa Valley of California to tour the two campuses of the Culinary Institute of America, well-known as one of the finest culinary teaching institutions in the world. The tours include everything a culinary student could desire—a multitude of magnificent buildings, breathtaking kitchens, well-stocked libraries and an assortment of fine restaurants where newly learned skills can be tested. What is harder to absorb on just a tour, however, is the quality and dedication of the teachers, here called "chef-instructors," who are what really make those brick buildings a world-class culinary college. Teachers who, on a daily basis, train thousands of students in many different areas of the culinary arts, whether they are headed for a management position at a restaurant chain or to become a three-star chef, or just home cooks trying to improve their skills.

You can find those chef-instructors in our public television series, *Cooking Secrets of the CIA*, on which this book is based. Season after season, they have maintained a strong connection to the millions of invisible viewers who tune in week after week wanting to get a glimpse of how the pros do it. They have given public television viewers important and useful cooking skills, not to mention great-tasting recipes. They have graciously endured the hardships of filming a cooking lesson, which has been likened to "cooking in traffic."

They are a tremendous group and I would like to personally acknowledge each and every one of them: Wayne L. Almquist, Elizabeth Briggs, Robert Briggs, Bill Briwa, Ronald DeSantis, C.M.C, Joseph DiPerri, Victor Gielisse, CM.C., James W. Heywood, Joseph McKenna, C.M.P.C., Stacy Radin, William Reynolds, Timothy Rodgers, and Fritz Sonnenschmidt, C.M.C.

Besides our "stars," we are very grateful to our lead sponsor, Cuisinart, who has now sponsored *Cooking Secrets* for four seasons, supporting the project when it was a mere concept on paper. Cuisinart understand that a great number of people not only want equipment which is every bit as good as what professionals use, but also want to learn cooking skills from real professionals. We are especially grateful to Lee Rizzuto, Barry Haber, Paul Ackels, and Mary Rodgers for their ongoing support.

Another sponsor to whom we are very grateful is the Weber-Stephen Products Company, whose grills have become the centerpieces of millions of American backyards. Weber, along with our CIA chefs, has proven that grilling goes way beyond steaks, chicken and hamburgers.

A big thank you also to our sponsor, the International Olive Oil Council. Just as Joe DiPerri, one of our Italian chef-instructors, regularly "blesses" his finished dishes with a drizzle of rich olive oil, we feel blessed to have their participation in this project.

It is often said that you eat with your eyes first and since our viewers can't taste our food, we are always on the lookout for beautiful plates and serving dishes to use in the programs. We are very grateful to the companies who have provided us with the many props needed to produce a series like this. They include Oneida, Villeroy & Boch, Wilton Armetale, Steelite, Sasaki, Hausenware, Emile Henry, Chicago Metallic and Majilly, Catskill Craftsmen, and Cost Plus World Market.

Finally, we'd like to thank Beaulieu Vineyards in the Napa Valley for their great help and support with the project.

— Alec Fatalevich, Marjorie Poore, Producers

Cooking at the CIA ©1999 by Marjorie Poore Productions and the Culinary Institute of America

Photography: Alec Fatalevich

Design: Kari Perin, Perin+Perin

Editing: Jennifer Newens

Production: Kristen Wurz

ISBN 0-9651095-6-9

Printed in Hong Kong through Global Interprint, Santa Rosa, California

10 9 8 7 6 5 4 3 2 1

MPP Books, 363 14th Avenue, San Francisco, CA 94118

Cuisinart is proud to sponsor Public Broadcasting's "Cooking Secrets of The CIA".

When Cuisinart introduced home cooks to the world-famous food processor, we shared a secret professional cooks had known for years.

Today, we continue to strive for culinary excellence, and this is why we are pleased to be part of "Cooking Secrets of The CIA".

The Culinary Institute of America dedicates itself to provide the finest culinary education in the world.

Cuisinart
Pro Food Prep Center

ON   OFF-PULSE

Cuisinart

Cuisinart® Professional Series Food Processors

Simplify your life and make cooking a pleasure. The Cuisinart® Pro Food Prep Center does it all – from salads and pasta sauce to pizza dough and cookies. Precise enough for small quantities and large enough to help you feed a crowd, the Pro Food Prep Center comes with everything you need to make great meals. Includes our exclusive large feed tube, compact cover, slicing and shredding discs and chopping blade – all dishwasher safe – plus a handy how-to video.

SmartStick® Extendable Hand Blender

Leave it to Cuisinart to extend your blending options! Our SmartStick® Extendable Shaft Hand Blender features an adjustable shaft that easily extends to reach deep into big pots of soup and sauces and into the very bottom of tall pitchers. Four speeds, plus our handy Mini-Prep™ chopper/grinder, a whipping disc and a chopping blade, further extend your food prep options.

SmartPower™ CountUp™ 9-Speed Electronic Hand Mixer

This is the mixer you can count on. Literally! A digital timer, built right into an exceptionally comfortable handle, starts running the instant you start mixing. You'll never over – or under – mix again. With 220 watts, automatic feedback power that kicks in when needed, 9 speeds (including 3 extra low and a really Smooth Start™), plus a chef's whisk, you'll find there's very little this mixer can't handle!

SmartPower™ 7-Speed Electronic Blender

This SmartPower™ sets a new standard in blending. A powerful motor is strong enough to crush ice without liquid, yet precise enough to mince delicate herbs. The 40-ounce glass jar with dripless spout holds enough drinks, salsa or soup for a crowd. Easy-to-clean touchpad, pulse control, one-touch ice crushing, and a design chosen best by consumers make this blender a very smart choice.

Custom Control™ Total Touch® Toaster

Smooth lines and user-friendly features make this premium Cuisinart® toaster a perfect fit for every lifestyle. It toasts everything from whole bagels to the thinnest breads and looks good while doing it! Perfect toast is guaranteed with special settings like 1-Slice Single Select and Bagel Buttons, as well as Defrost and Reheat controls. And Your Choice™ Browning Memory will remember just how you like it!

Coffee Bar™ 10-Cup Automatic Grind & Brew

Coffee doesn't come any fresher than this! The Grind & Brew automatically grinds beans and brews the freshest coffee in one easy step. Our exclusive brewing process is the same used by the best coffee bars, so coffee is flavorful and delicious. And the patented Taste-Keeper™ Lid keeps oxygen out so coffee stays fresh for hours. Programmable start, automatic shutoff, self-clean function...great coffee doesn't get any easier than this!

Cuisinart

Cuisinart® Everyday Collection® Cookware

Originally inspired by great chefs, Cuisinart® Everyday Collection® Cookware is as rugged as it is beautiful. Its 18/10 mirror-finish stainless steel with copper bottom construction cooks better and faster. Stay-cool handles, a stick-resistant cooking surface and easy dishwasher cleanup make Cuisinart® cookware a pleasure to own and to use.

Anodized Non-Stick Cookware

This cookware offers the best of both worlds: The superior performance of aluminum – and cooking surfaces that are 100% aluminum-free! Cuisinart uses heavy gauge anodized aluminum – the exterior polished to a rich, dark finish, the inner core reinforcing the metal's quick and even heat conduction. The 100% aluminum-free cooking surface is internally reinforced and nonstick. It provides lifetime food release for healthy, oil-free cooking and easy cleanups. Take it from the range to the oven to the table. With solid stainless steel lids and beautifully contoured handles that stay cool on the stovetop, it is cookware that looks as good as it cooks.

Cuisinart® Stick Free
Stainless Non-Stick Cookware

Cuisinart has combined nonstick convenience with professional quality cookware, setting a new standard in nonstick cookware. It contains no aluminum and is designed for flavorful, healthful cooking. Through a special Excalibur® Multi-Layer System, stainless steel is actually built into the nonstick material for superior durability.